C-3635   CAREER EXAMINATION SERIES

This is your
PASSBOOK for...

Home Health Aide

Test Preparation Study Guide
Questions & Answers

NATIONAL LEARNING CORPORATION®

COPYRIGHT NOTICE

This book is SOLELY intended for, is sold ONLY to, and its use is RESTRICTED to individual, bona fide applicants or candidates who qualify by virtue of having seriously filed applications for appropriate license, certificate, professional and/or promotional advancement, higher school matriculation, scholarship, or other legitimate requirements of education and/or governmental authorities.

This book is NOT intended for use, class instruction, tutoring, training, duplication, copying, reprinting, excerption, or adaptation, etc., by:

1) Other publishers
2) Proprietors and/or Instructors of "Coaching" and/or Preparatory Courses
3) Personnel and/or Training Divisions of commercial, industrial, and governmental organizations
4) Schools, colleges, or universities and/or their departments and staffs, including teachers and other personnel
5) Testing Agencies or Bureaus
6) Study groups which seek by the purchase of a single volume to copy and/or duplicate and/or adapt this material for use by the group as a whole without having purchased individual volumes for each of the members of the group
7) Et al.

Such persons would be in violation of appropriate Federal and State statutes.

PROVISION OF LICENSING AGREEMENTS – Recognized educational, commercial, industrial, and governmental institutions and organizations, and others legitimately engaged in educational pursuits, including training, testing, and measurement activities, may address request for a licensing agreement to the copyright owners, who will determine whether, and under what conditions, including fees and charges, the materials in this book may be used them. In other words, a licensing facility exists for the legitimate use of the material in this book on other than an individual basis. However, it is asseverated and affirmed here that the material in this book CANNOT be used without the receipt of the express permission of such a licensing agreement from the Publishers. Inquiries re licensing should be addressed to the company, attention rights and permissions department.

All rights reserved, including the right of reproduction in whole or in part, in any form or by any means, electronic or mechanical, including photocopying, recording, or by any information storage and retrieval system, without permission in writing from the Publisher.

Copyright © 2024 by
National Learning Corporation

212 Michael Drive, Syosset, NY 11791
(516) 921-8888 • www.passbooks.com
E-mail: info@passbooks.com

PASSBOOK® SERIES

THE *PASSBOOK® SERIES* has been created to prepare applicants and candidates for the ultimate academic battlefield – the examination room.

At some time in our lives, each and every one of us may be required to take an examination – for validation, matriculation, admission, qualification, registration, certification, or licensure.

Based on the assumption that every applicant or candidate has met the basic formal educational standards, has taken the required number of courses, and read the necessary texts, the *PASSBOOK® SERIES* furnishes the one special preparation which may assure passing with confidence, instead of failing with insecurity. Examination questions – together with answers – are furnished as the basic vehicle for study so that the mysteries of the examination and its compounding difficulties may be eliminated or diminished by a sure method.

This book is meant to help you pass your examination provided that you qualify and are serious in your objective.

The entire field is reviewed through the huge store of content information which is succinctly presented through a provocative and challenging approach – the question-and-answer method.

A climate of success is established by furnishing the correct answers at the end of each test.

You soon learn to recognize types of questions, forms of questions, and patterns of questioning. You may even begin to anticipate expected outcomes.

You perceive that many questions are repeated or adapted so that you can gain acute insights, which may enable you to score many sure points.

You learn how to confront new questions, or types of questions, and to attack them confidently and work out the correct answers.

You note objectives and emphases, and recognize pitfalls and dangers, so that you may make positive educational adjustments.

Moreover, you are kept fully informed in relation to new concepts, methods, practices, and directions in the field.

You discover that you are actually taking the examination all the time: you are preparing for the examination by "taking" an examination, not by reading extraneous and/or supererogatory textbooks.

In short, this PASSBOOK®, used directedly, should be an important factor in helping you to pass your test.

HOME HEALTH AIDES
PERSONAL AND HOME CARE AIDES

Significant Points

- Job opportunities are expected to be excellent because of rapid growth in home healthcare and high replacement needs.
- Training requirements vary from State to State, the type of home services agency, and funding source covering the costs of services.
- Many of these workers work part time and weekends or evenings to suit the needs of their clients.

Nature of the Work

Home health aides and personal and home care aides help people who are disabled, chronically ill, or cognitively impaired and older adults, who may need assistance, live in their own homes or in residential facilities instead of in health facilities or institutions. They also assist people in hospices and day programs and help individuals with disabilities go to work and remain engaged in their communities. Most aides work with elderly or physically or mentally disabled clients who need more care than family or friends can provide. Others help discharge hospital patients who have relatively short-term needs.

Aides provide light housekeeping and homemaking tasks such as laundry, change bed linens, shop for food, plan and prepare meals. Aides also may help clients get out of bed, bathe, dress, and groom. Some accompany clients to doctors' appointments or on other errands.

Home health aides and personal and home care aides provide instruction and psychological support to their clients. They may advise families and patients on nutrition, cleanliness, and household tasks.

Aides' daily routine may vary. They may go to the same home every day or week for months or even years and often visit four or five clients on the same day. However, some aides may work solely with one client who is in need of more care and attention. In some situations, this may involve working with other aides in shifts so that the client has an aide throughout the day and night. Aides also work with clients, particularly younger adults at schools or at the client's work site.

In general, home health aides and personal and home care aides have similar job duties. However, there are some small differences.

Home health aides typically work for certified home health or hospice agencies that receive government funding and therefore must comply with regulations from to receive funding. This means that they must work under the direct supervision of a medical professional, usually a nurse. These aides keep records of services performed and of clients' condition and progress. They report changes in the client's condition to the supervisor or case manager. Aides also work with therapists and other medical staff.

Home health aides may provide some basic health-related services, such as checking patients' pulse rate, temperature, and respiration rate. They also may help with simple prescribed exercises and assist with medications administration. Occasionally, they change simple dressings, give massages, provide skin care, or assist with braces and artificial limbs.

With special training, experienced home health aides also may assist with medical equipment such as ventilators, which help patients breathe.

Personal and home care aides-also called homemakers, caregivers, companions, and personal attendants-work for various public and private agencies that provide home care services. In these agencies, caregivers are likely supervised by a licensed nurse, social worker, or other non-medical managers. Aides receive detailed instructions explaining when to visit clients and what services to perform for them.

However, personal and home care aides work independently, with only periodic visits by their supervis These caregivers may work with only one client each day or five or six clients once a day every week or every 2 weeks.

Some aides are hired directly by the patient or the patient's family. In these situations, personal and home care aides are supervised and assigned tasks directly by the patient or the patient's family.

Aides may also work with individuals who are developmentally or intellectually disabled. These workers are often called direct support professionals and they may assist in implementing a behavior plan, teaching self-care skills and providing employment support, as well as providing a range of other personal assistance services

Work environment
Work as an aide can be physically demanding. Aides must guard against back injury because they may have to move patients into and out of bed or help them to stand or walk. Aides also may face hazards from minor infections and exposure to communicable diseases, such as hepatitis, but can avoid infections by following proper procedures. Because mechanical lifting devices available in institutional settings are not as frequently available in patients' homes, home health aides must take extra care to avoid injuries resulting from overexertion when they assist patients. These workers experienced a larger than average number of work-related injuries or illnesses.

Aides also perform tasks that some may consider unpleasant, such as emptying bedpans and changing soiled bed linens. The patients they care for may be disoriented, irritable, or uncooperative. Although their work can be emotionally demanding, many aides gain satisfaction from assisting those in need

Most aides work with a number of different patients, each job lasting a few hours, days, or weeks. They often visit multiple patients on the same day. Surroundings differ by case. Some homes are neat and pleasant, whereas others are untidy and depressing. Some clients are pleasant and cooperative; others are angry, abusive, depressed, or otherwise difficult.

Home health aides and personal and home care aides generally work alone, with periodic visits from their supervisor. They receive detailed instructions explaining when to visit patients and what services to perform. Aides are responsible for getting to patients' homes, and they may spend a good portion of the work day traveling from one patient to another.

Many of these workers work part time and weekends or evenings to suit the needs of their clients.

Training, Other Qualifications, and Advancement
Home health aides must receive formal training and pass a competency test to work for certified home health or hospice agencies that receive reimbursement from Medicare or Medicaid. Personal and home care aides, however, face a wide range of requirements, which vary from State to State.

Education and training. Home health aides and personal and home care aides are generally not required to have a high school diploma. They usually are trained on the job by registered nurses, licensed practical nurses, experienced aides, or their supervisor. Aides are instructed on how to cook for a client, including on special diets. Furthermore, they may be trained in basic housekeeping tasks, such as making a bed and keeping the home sanitary and safe for the client. Generally, they are taught how to respond to an emergency, learning basic safety techniques. Employers also may train aides to conduct themselves in a professional and courteous manner while in a client's home. Some clients prefer that tasks are done a certain way and will teach the aide. A competency evaluation may be required to ensure that the aide can perform the required tasks.

Licensure
Home health aides who work for agencies that receive reimbursement from Medicare or Medicaid must receive a minimum level of training. They must complete both a training program consisting of a minimum of 75 hours and a competency evaluation or state certification program. Training includes information regarding personal hygiene, safe transfer techniques, reading and recording vital signs, infection control, and basic nutrition. Aides may take a competency exam to become certified without taking any of the training. At a minimum, 16 hours of supervised practical training are required before an aide has direct contact with a resident. These certification requirements represent the minimum, as outlined by the Federal Government. Some States may require additional hours of training to become certified.

Personal and home care aides are not required to be certified.

Other qualifications. Aides should have a desire to help people. They should be responsible, compassionate, patient, emotionally stable, and cheerful. In addition, aides should be tactful, honest, and discreet, because they work in private homes. Aides also must be in good health.
A physical examination, including State-mandated tests for tuberculosis and other diseases, may be required. A criminal background check and a good driving record also may be required for employment.

Certification and advancement. The National Association for Home Care and Hospice (NAHC) offers national certification for aides. Certification is a voluntary demonstration that the individual has met industry standards. Certification requires the completion of 75 hours of training; observation and documentation of 17 skills for competency, assessed by a registered nurse; and the passing of a written exam developed by NAHC.

Advancement for home health aides and personal and home care aides is limited. In some agencies, workers start out performing homemaker duties, such as cleaning. With experience and training, they may take on more personal care duties. Some aides choose to receive additional training to become nursing aides, licensed practical nurses, or registered nurses. Some may start their own home care agency or work as a self-employed aide. Self-employed aides have no agency affiliation or supervision and accept clients, set fees, and arrange work schedules on their own.

Employment
Home health aides and personal and home care aides hold about 1.7 million jobs. The majority of jobs were in home healthcare services, individual and family services, residential care facilities, and private households.

Job Outlook
Excellent job opportunities are expected for this occupation because rapid employment growth and high replacement needs are projected to produce a large number of job openings.

Employment change. Employment of home health aides is projected to grow by 50 percent by 2020, which is much faster than the average for all occupations. Employment of personal and home care aides is also expected to grow by 50 percent by 2020, which is much faster than the average for all occupations. For both occupations, the expected growth is due, in large part, to the projected rise in the number of elderly people, an age group that often has mounting health problems and that needs some assistance with daily activities. The elderly and other clients, such as the mentally disabled, increasingly rely on home care.

This trend reflects several developments. Inpatient care in hospitals and nursing homes can be extremely expensive, so more patients return to their homes from these facilities as quickly as possible in order to contain costs. Patients, who need assistance with everyday tasks and household chores rather than medical care, can reduce medical expenses by returning to their homes. Furthermore, most patients--particularly the elderly--prefer care in their homes rather than in nursing homes or other in-patient facilities. This development is aided by the realization that treatment can be more effective in familiar surroundings.

Job prospects. In addition to job openings created by the increased demand for these workers, replacement needs are expected to lead to many openings. The relatively low skill requirements, low pay, and high emotional demands of the work result in high replacement needs. For these same reasons, many people are reluctant to seek jobs in the occupation. Therefore, persons who are interested in and suited for this work--particularly those with experience or training as personal care, home health, or nursing aides--should have excellent job prospects.

HOW TO TAKE A TEST

I. YOU MUST PASS AN EXAMINATION

A. WHAT EVERY CANDIDATE SHOULD KNOW

Examination applicants often ask us for help in preparing for the written test. What can I study in advance? What kinds of questions will be asked? How will the test be given? How will the papers be graded?

As an applicant for a civil service examination, you may be wondering about some of these things. Our purpose here is to suggest effective methods of advance study and to describe civil service examinations.

Your chances for success on this examination can be increased if you know how to prepare. Those "pre-examination jitters" can be reduced if you know what to expect. You can even experience an adventure in good citizenship if you know why civil service exams are given.

B. WHY ARE CIVIL SERVICE EXAMINATIONS GIVEN?

Civil service examinations are important to you in two ways. As a citizen, you want public jobs filled by employees who know how to do their work. As a job seeker, you want a fair chance to compete for that job on an equal footing with other candidates. The best-known means of accomplishing this two-fold goal is the competitive examination.

Exams are widely publicized throughout the nation. They may be administered for jobs in federal, state, city, municipal, town or village governments or agencies.

Any citizen may apply, with some limitations, such as the age or residence of applicants. Your experience and education may be reviewed to see whether you meet the requirements for the particular examination. When these requirements exist, they are reasonable and applied consistently to all applicants. Thus, a competitive examination may cause you some uneasiness now, but it is your privilege and safeguard.

C. HOW ARE CIVIL SERVICE EXAMS DEVELOPED?

Examinations are carefully written by trained technicians who are specialists in the field known as "psychological measurement," in consultation with recognized authorities in the field of work that the test will cover. These experts recommend the subject matter areas or skills to be tested; only those knowledges or skills important to your success on the job are included. The most reliable books and source materials available are used as references. Together, the experts and technicians judge the difficulty level of the questions.

Test technicians know how to phrase questions so that the problem is clearly stated. Their ethics do not permit "trick" or "catch" questions. Questions may have been tried out on sample groups, or subjected to statistical analysis, to determine their usefulness.

Written tests are often used in combination with performance tests, ratings of training and experience, and oral interviews. All of these measures combine to form the best-known means of finding the right person for the right job.

II. HOW TO PASS THE WRITTEN TEST

A. NATURE OF THE EXAMINATION

To prepare intelligently for civil service examinations, you should know how they differ from school examinations you have taken. In school you were assigned certain definite pages to read or subjects to cover. The examination questions were quite detailed and usually emphasized memory. Civil service exams, on the other hand, try to discover your present ability to perform the duties of a position, plus your potentiality to learn these duties. In other words, a civil service exam attempts to predict how successful you will be. Questions cover such a broad area that they cannot be as minute and detailed as school exam questions.

In the public service similar kinds of work, or positions, are grouped together in one "class." This process is known as *position-classification*. All the positions in a class are paid according to the salary range for that class. One class title covers all of these positions, and they are all tested by the same examination.

B. FOUR BASIC STEPS

1) Study the announcement

How, then, can you know what subjects to study? Our best answer is: "Learn as much as possible about the class of positions for which you've applied." The exam will test the knowledge, skills and abilities needed to do the work.

Your most valuable source of information about the position you want is the official exam announcement. This announcement lists the training and experience qualifications. Check these standards and apply only if you come reasonably close to meeting them.

The brief description of the position in the examination announcement offers some clues to the subjects which will be tested. Think about the job itself. Review the duties in your mind. Can you perform them, or are there some in which you are rusty? Fill in the blank spots in your preparation.

Many jurisdictions preview the written test in the exam announcement by including a section called "Knowledge and Abilities Required," "Scope of the Examination," or some similar heading. Here you will find out specifically what fields will be tested.

2) Review your own background

Once you learn in general what the position is all about, and what you need to know to do the work, ask yourself which subjects you already know fairly well and which need improvement. You may wonder whether to concentrate on improving your strong areas or on building some background in your fields of weakness. When the announcement has specified "some knowledge" or "considerable knowledge," or has used adjectives like "beginning principles of..." or "advanced ... methods," you can get a clue as to the number and difficulty of questions to be asked in any given field. More questions, and hence broader coverage, would be included for those subjects which are more important in the work. Now weigh your strengths and weaknesses against the job requirements and prepare accordingly.

3) Determine the level of the position

Another way to tell how intensively you should prepare is to understand the level of the job for which you are applying. Is it the entering level? In other words, is this the position in which beginners in a field of work are hired? Or is it an intermediate or advanced level? Sometimes this is indicated by such words as "Junior" or "Senior" in the class title. Other jurisdictions use Roman numerals to designate the level – Clerk I, Clerk II, for example. The word "Supervisor" sometimes appears in the title. If the level is not indicated by the title, check the description of duties. Will you be working under very close supervision, or will you have responsibility for independent decisions in this work?

4) Choose appropriate study materials

Now that you know the subjects to be examined and the relative amount of each subject to be covered, you can choose suitable study materials. For beginning level jobs, or even advanced ones, if you have a pronounced weakness in some aspect of your training, read a modern, standard textbook in that field. Be sure it is up to date and has general coverage. Such books are normally available at your library, and the librarian will be glad to help you locate one. For entry-level positions, questions of appropriate difficulty are chosen – neither highly advanced questions, nor those too simple. Such questions require careful thought but not advanced training.

If the position for which you are applying is technical or advanced, you will read more advanced, specialized material. If you are already familiar with the basic principles of your field, elementary textbooks would waste your time. Concentrate on advanced textbooks and technical periodicals. Think through the concepts and review difficult problems in your field.

These are all general sources. You can get more ideas on your own initiative, following these leads. For example, training manuals and publications of the government agency which employs workers in your field can be useful, particularly for technical and professional positions. A letter or visit to the government department involved may result in more specific study suggestions, and certainly will provide you with a more definite idea of the exact nature of the position you are seeking.

III. KINDS OF TESTS

Tests are used for purposes other than measuring knowledge and ability to perform specified duties. For some positions, it is equally important to test ability to make adjustments to new situations or to profit from training. In others, basic mental abilities not dependent on information are essential. Questions which test these things may not appear as pertinent to the duties of the position as those which test for knowledge and information. Yet they are often highly important parts of a fair examination. For very general questions, it is almost impossible to help you direct your study efforts. What we can do is to point out some of the more common of these general abilities needed in public service positions and describe some typical questions.

1) General information

Broad, general information has been found useful for predicting job success in some kinds of work. This is tested in a variety of ways, from vocabulary lists to questions about current events. Basic background in some field of work, such as sociology or economics, may be sampled in a group of questions. Often these are principles which have become familiar to most persons through exposure rather than through formal training. It is difficult to advise you how to study for these questions; being alert to the world around you is our best suggestion.

2) Verbal ability

An example of an ability needed in many positions is verbal or language ability. Verbal ability is, in brief, the ability to use and understand words. Vocabulary and grammar tests are typical measures of this ability. Reading comprehension or paragraph interpretation questions are common in many kinds of civil service tests. You are given a paragraph of written material and asked to find its central meaning.

3) Numerical ability

Number skills can be tested by the familiar arithmetic problem, by checking paired lists of numbers to see which are alike and which are different, or by interpreting charts and graphs. In the latter test, a graph may be printed in the test booklet which you are asked to use as the basis for answering questions.

4) Observation

A popular test for law-enforcement positions is the observation test. A picture is shown to you for several minutes, then taken away. Questions about the picture test your ability to observe both details and larger elements.

5) Following directions

In many positions in the public service, the employee must be able to carry out written instructions dependably and accurately. You may be given a chart with several columns, each column listing a variety of information. The questions require you to carry out directions involving the information given in the chart.

6) Skills and aptitudes

Performance tests effectively measure some manual skills and aptitudes. When the skill is one in which you are trained, such as typing or shorthand, you can practice. These tests are often very much like those given in business school or high school courses. For many of the other skills and aptitudes, however, no short-time preparation can be made. Skills and abilities natural to you or that you have developed throughout your lifetime are being tested.

Many of the general questions just described provide all the data needed to answer the questions and ask you to use your reasoning ability to find the answers. Your best preparation for these tests, as well as for tests of facts and ideas, is to be at your physical and mental best. You, no doubt, have your own methods of getting into an exam-taking mood and keeping "in shape." The next section lists some ideas on this subject.

IV. KINDS OF QUESTIONS

Only rarely is the "essay" question, which you answer in narrative form, used in civil service tests. Civil service tests are usually of the short-answer type. Full instructions for answering these questions will be given to you at the examination. But in case this is your first experience with short-answer questions and separate answer sheets, here is what you need to know:

1) Multiple-choice Questions

Most popular of the short-answer questions is the "multiple choice" or "best answer" question. It can be used, for example, to test for factual knowledge, ability to solve problems or judgment in meeting situations found at work.

A multiple-choice question is normally one of three types—
- It can begin with an incomplete statement followed by several possible endings. You are to find the one ending which *best* completes the statement, although some of the others may not be entirely wrong.
- It can also be a complete statement in the form of a question which is answered by choosing one of the statements listed.

- It can be in the form of a problem – again you select the best answer.

Here is an example of a multiple-choice question with a discussion which should give you some clues as to the method for choosing the right answer:

When an employee has a complaint about his assignment, the action which will *best* help him overcome his difficulty is to
- A. discuss his difficulty with his coworkers
- B. take the problem to the head of the organization
- C. take the problem to the person who gave him the assignment
- D. say nothing to anyone about his complaint

In answering this question, you should study each of the choices to find which is best. Consider choice "A" – Certainly an employee may discuss his complaint with fellow employees, but no change or improvement can result, and the complaint remains unresolved. Choice "B" is a poor choice since the head of the organization probably does not know what assignment you have been given, and taking your problem to him is known as "going over the head" of the supervisor. The supervisor, or person who made the assignment, is the person who can clarify it or correct any injustice. Choice "C" is, therefore, correct. To say nothing, as in choice "D," is unwise. Supervisors have and interest in knowing the problems employees are facing, and the employee is seeking a solution to his problem.

2) True/False Questions

The "true/false" or "right/wrong" form of question is sometimes used. Here a complete statement is given. Your job is to decide whether the statement is right or wrong.

SAMPLE: A roaming cell-phone call to a nearby city costs less than a non-roaming call to a distant city.

This statement is wrong, or false, since roaming calls are more expensive.

This is not a complete list of all possible question forms, although most of the others are variations of these common types. You will always get complete directions for answering questions. Be sure you understand *how* to mark your answers – ask questions until you do.

V. RECORDING YOUR ANSWERS

Computer terminals are used more and more today for many different kinds of exams.
For an examination with very few applicants, you may be told to record your answers in the test booklet itself. Separate answer sheets are much more common. If this separate answer sheet is to be scored by machine – and this is often the case – it is highly important that you mark your answers correctly in order to get credit.

An electronic scoring machine is often used in civil service offices because of the speed with which papers can be scored. Machine-scored answer sheets must be marked with a pencil, which will be given to you. This pencil has a high graphite content which responds to the electronic scoring machine. As a matter of fact, stray dots may register as answers, so do not let your pencil rest on the answer sheet while you are pondering the correct answer. Also, if your pencil lead breaks or is otherwise defective, ask for another.

Since the answer sheet will be dropped in a slot in the scoring machine, be careful not to bend the corners or get the paper crumpled.

The answer sheet normally has five vertical columns of numbers, with 30 numbers to a column. These numbers correspond to the question numbers in your test booklet. After each number, going across the page are four or five pairs of dotted lines. These short dotted lines have small letters or numbers above them. The first two pairs may also have a "T" or "F" above the letters. This indicates that the first two pairs only are to be used if the questions are of the true-false type. If the questions are multiple choice, disregard the "T" and "F" and pay attention only to the small letters or numbers.

Answer your questions in the manner of the sample that follows:

32. The largest city in the United States is
    A. Washington, D.C.
    B. New York City
    C. Chicago
    D. Detroit
    E. San Francisco

1) Choose the answer you think is best. (New York City is the largest, so "B" is correct.)
2) Find the row of dotted lines numbered the same as the question you are answering. (Find row number 32)
3) Find the pair of dotted lines corresponding to the answer. (Find the pair of lines under the mark "B.")
4) Make a solid black mark between the dotted lines.

VI. BEFORE THE TEST

Common sense will help you find procedures to follow to get ready for an examination. Too many of us, however, overlook these sensible measures. Indeed, nervousness and fatigue have been found to be the most serious reasons why applicants fail to do their best on civil service tests. Here is a list of reminders:

- Begin your preparation early – Don't wait until the last minute to go scurrying around for books and materials or to find out what the position is all about.
- Prepare continuously – An hour a night for a week is better than an all-night cram session. This has been definitely established. What is more, a night a week for a month will return better dividends than crowding your study into a shorter period of time.
- Locate the place of the exam – You have been sent a notice telling you when and where to report for the examination. If the location is in a different town or otherwise unfamiliar to you, it would be well to inquire the best route and learn something about the building.
- Relax the night before the test – Allow your mind to rest. Do not study at all that night. Plan some mild recreation or diversion; then go to bed early and get a good night's sleep.
- Get up early enough to make a leisurely trip to the place for the test – This way unforeseen events, traffic snarls, unfamiliar buildings, etc. will not upset you.
- Dress comfortably – A written test is not a fashion show. You will be known by number and not by name, so wear something comfortable.

- Leave excess paraphernalia at home – Shopping bags and odd bundles will get in your way. You need bring only the items mentioned in the official notice you received; usually everything you need is provided. Do not bring reference books to the exam. They will only confuse those last minutes and be taken away from you when in the test room.
- Arrive somewhat ahead of time – If because of transportation schedules you must get there very early, bring a newspaper or magazine to take your mind off yourself while waiting.
- Locate the examination room – When you have found the proper room, you will be directed to the seat or part of the room where you will sit. Sometimes you are given a sheet of instructions to read while you are waiting. Do not fill out any forms until you are told to do so; just read them and be prepared.
- Relax and prepare to listen to the instructions
- If you have any physical problem that may keep you from doing your best, be sure to tell the test administrator. If you are sick or in poor health, you really cannot do your best on the exam. You can come back and take the test some other time.

VII. AT THE TEST

The day of the test is here and you have the test booklet in your hand. The temptation to get going is very strong. Caution! There is more to success than knowing the right answers. You must know how to identify your papers and understand variations in the type of short-answer question used in this particular examination. Follow these suggestions for maximum results from your efforts:

1) Cooperate with the monitor

The test administrator has a duty to create a situation in which you can be as much at ease as possible. He will give instructions, tell you when to begin, check to see that you are marking your answer sheet correctly, and so on. He is not there to guard you, although he will see that your competitors do not take unfair advantage. He wants to help you do your best.

2) Listen to all instructions

Don't jump the gun! Wait until you understand all directions. In most civil service tests you get more time than you need to answer the questions. So don't be in a hurry. Read each word of instructions until you clearly understand the meaning. Study the examples, listen to all announcements and follow directions. Ask questions if you do not understand what to do.

3) Identify your papers

Civil service exams are usually identified by number only. You will be assigned a number; you must not put your name on your test papers. Be sure to copy your number correctly. Since more than one exam may be given, copy your exact examination title.

4) Plan your time

Unless you are told that a test is a "speed" or "rate of work" test, speed itself is usually not important. Time enough to answer all the questions will be provided, but this does not mean that you have all day. An overall time limit has been set. Divide the total time (in minutes) by the number of questions to determine the approximate time you have for each question.

5) Do not linger over difficult questions
If you come across a difficult question, mark it with a paper clip (useful to have along) and come back to it when you have been through the booklet. One caution if you do this – be sure to skip a number on your answer sheet as well. Check often to be sure that you have not lost your place and that you are marking in the row numbered the same as the question you are answering.

6) Read the questions
Be sure you know what the question asks! Many capable people are unsuccessful because they failed to *read* the questions correctly.

7) Answer all questions
Unless you have been instructed that a penalty will be deducted for incorrect answers, it is better to guess than to omit a question.

8) Speed tests
It is often better NOT to guess on speed tests. It has been found that on timed tests people are tempted to spend the last few seconds before time is called in marking answers at random – without even reading them – in the hope of picking up a few extra points. To discourage this practice, the instructions may warn you that your score will be "corrected" for guessing. That is, a penalty will be applied. The incorrect answers will be deducted from the correct ones, or some other penalty formula will be used.

9) Review your answers
If you finish before time is called, go back to the questions you guessed or omitted to give them further thought. Review other answers if you have time.

10) Return your test materials
If you are ready to leave before others have finished or time is called, take ALL your materials to the monitor and leave quietly. Never take any test material with you. The monitor can discover whose papers are not complete, and taking a test booklet may be grounds for disqualification.

VIII. EXAMINATION TECHNIQUES

1) Read the general instructions carefully. These are usually printed on the first page of the exam booklet. As a rule, these instructions refer to the timing of the examination; the fact that you should not start work until the signal and must stop work at a signal, etc. If there are any *special* instructions, such as a choice of questions to be answered, make sure that you note this instruction carefully.

2) When you are ready to start work on the examination, that is as soon as the signal has been given, read the instructions to each question booklet, underline any key words or phrases, such as *least, best, outline, describe* and the like. In this way you will tend to answer as requested rather than discover on reviewing your paper that you *listed without describing*, that you selected the *worst* choice rather than the *best* choice, etc.

3) If the examination is of the objective or multiple-choice type – that is, each question will also give a series of possible answers: A, B, C or D, and you are called upon to select the best answer and write the letter next to that answer on your answer paper – it is advisable to start answering each question in turn. There may be anywhere from 50 to 100 such questions in the three or four hours allotted and you can see how much time would be taken if you read through all the questions before beginning to answer any. Furthermore, if you come across a question or group of questions which you know would be difficult to answer, it would undoubtedly affect your handling of all the other questions.

4) If the examination is of the essay type and contains but a few questions, it is a moot point as to whether you should read all the questions before starting to answer any one. Of course, if you are given a choice – say five out of seven and the like – then it is essential to read all the questions so you can eliminate the two that are most difficult. If, however, you are asked to answer all the questions, there may be danger in trying to answer the easiest one first because you may find that you will spend too much time on it. The best technique is to answer the first question, then proceed to the second, etc.

5) Time your answers. Before the exam begins, write down the time it started, then add the time allowed for the examination and write down the time it must be completed, then divide the time available somewhat as follows:
    - If 3-1/2 hours are allowed, that would be 210 minutes. If you have 80 objective-type questions, that would be an average of 2-1/2 minutes per question. Allow yourself no more than 2 minutes per question, or a total of 160 minutes, which will permit about 50 minutes to review.
    - If for the time allotment of 210 minutes there are 7 essay questions to answer, that would average about 30 minutes a question. Give yourself only 25 minutes per question so that you have about 35 minutes to review.

6) The most important instruction is to *read each question* and make sure you know what is wanted. The second most important instruction is to *time yourself properly* so that you answer every question. The third most important instruction is to *answer every question*. Guess if you have to but include something for each question. Remember that you will receive no credit for a blank and will probably receive some credit if you write something in answer to an essay question. If you guess a letter – say "B" for a multiple-choice question – you may have guessed right. If you leave a blank as an answer to a multiple-choice question, the examiners may respect your feelings but it will not add a point to your score. Some exams may penalize you for wrong answers, so in such cases *only*, you may not want to guess unless you have some basis for your answer.

7) Suggestions
    a. Objective-type questions
        1. Examine the question booklet for proper sequence of pages and questions
        2. Read all instructions carefully
        3. Skip any question which seems too difficult; return to it after all other questions have been answered
        4. Apportion your time properly; do not spend too much time on any single question or group of questions

5. Note and underline key words – *all, most, fewest, least, best, worst, same, opposite*, etc.
6. Pay particular attention to negatives
7. Note unusual option, e.g., unduly long, short, complex, different or similar in content to the body of the question
8. Observe the use of "hedging" words – *probably, may, most likely*, etc.
9. Make sure that your answer is put next to the same number as the question
10. Do not second-guess unless you have good reason to believe the second answer is definitely more correct
11. Cross out original answer if you decide another answer is more accurate; do not erase until you are ready to hand your paper in
12. Answer all questions; guess unless instructed otherwise
13. Leave time for review

   b. Essay questions
      1. Read each question carefully
      2. Determine exactly what is wanted. Underline key words or phrases.
      3. Decide on outline or paragraph answer
      4. Include many different points and elements unless asked to develop any one or two points or elements
      5. Show impartiality by giving pros and cons unless directed to select one side only
      6. Make and write down any assumptions you find necessary to answer the questions
      7. Watch your English, grammar, punctuation and choice of words
      8. Time your answers; don't crowd material

8) Answering the essay question

Most essay questions can be answered by framing the specific response around several key words or ideas. Here are a few such key words or ideas:

M's: manpower, materials, methods, money, management
P's: purpose, program, policy, plan, procedure, practice, problems, pitfalls, personnel, public relations

   a. Six basic steps in handling problems:
      1. Preliminary plan and background development
      2. Collect information, data and facts
      3. Analyze and interpret information, data and facts
      4. Analyze and develop solutions as well as make recommendations
      5. Prepare report and sell recommendations
      6. Install recommendations and follow up effectiveness

   b. Pitfalls to avoid
      1. *Taking things for granted* – A statement of the situation does not necessarily imply that each of the elements is necessarily true; for example, a complaint may be invalid and biased so that all that can be taken for granted is that a complaint has been registered

2. *Considering only one side of a situation* – Wherever possible, indicate several alternatives and then point out the reasons you selected the best one
3. *Failing to indicate follow up* – Whenever your answer indicates action on your part, make certain that you will take proper follow-up action to see how successful your recommendations, procedures or actions turn out to be
4. *Taking too long in answering any single question* – Remember to time your answers properly

IX. AFTER THE TEST

Scoring procedures differ in detail among civil service jurisdictions although the general principles are the same. Whether the papers are hand-scored or graded by machine we have described, they are nearly always graded by number. That is, the person who marks the paper knows only the number – never the name – of the applicant. Not until all the papers have been graded will they be matched with names. If other tests, such as training and experience or oral interview ratings have been given, scores will be combined. Different parts of the examination usually have different weights. For example, the written test might count 60 percent of the final grade, and a rating of training and experience 40 percent. In many jurisdictions, veterans will have a certain number of points added to their grades.

After the final grade has been determined, the names are placed in grade order and an eligible list is established. There are various methods for resolving ties between those who get the same final grade – probably the most common is to place first the name of the person whose application was received first. Job offers are made from the eligible list in the order the names appear on it. You will be notified of your grade and your rank as soon as all these computations have been made. This will be done as rapidly as possible.

People who are found to meet the requirements in the announcement are called "eligibles." Their names are put on a list of eligible candidates. An eligible's chances of getting a job depend on how high he stands on this list and how fast agencies are filling jobs from the list.

When a job is to be filled from a list of eligibles, the agency asks for the names of people on the list of eligibles for that job. When the civil service commission receives this request, it sends to the agency the names of the three people highest on this list. Or, if the job to be filled has specialized requirements, the office sends the agency the names of the top three persons who meet these requirements from the general list.

The appointing officer makes a choice from among the three people whose names were sent to him. If the selected person accepts the appointment, the names of the others are put back on the list to be considered for future openings.

That is the rule in hiring from all kinds of eligible lists, whether they are for typist, carpenter, chemist, or something else. For every vacancy, the appointing officer has his choice of any one of the top three eligibles on the list. This explains why the person whose name is on top of the list sometimes does not get an appointment when some of the persons lower on the list do. If the appointing officer chooses the second or third eligible, the No. 1 eligible does not get a job at once, but stays on the list until he is appointed or the list is terminated.

X. HOW TO PASS THE INTERVIEW TEST

The examination for which you applied requires an oral interview test. You have already taken the written test and you are now being called for the interview test – the final part of the formal examination.

You may think that it is not possible to prepare for an interview test and that there are no procedures to follow during an interview. Our purpose is to point out some things you can do in advance that will help you and some good rules to follow and pitfalls to avoid while you are being interviewed.

What is an interview supposed to test?

The written examination is designed to test the technical knowledge and competence of the candidate; the oral is designed to evaluate intangible qualities, not readily measured otherwise, and to establish a list showing the relative fitness of each candidate – as measured against his competitors – for the position sought. Scoring is not on the basis of "right" and "wrong," but on a sliding scale of values ranging from "not passable" to "outstanding." As a matter of fact, it is possible to achieve a relatively low score without a single "incorrect" answer because of evident weakness in the qualities being measured.

Occasionally, an examination may consist entirely of an oral test – either an individual or a group oral. In such cases, information is sought concerning the technical knowledges and abilities of the candidate, since there has been no written examination for this purpose. More commonly, however, an oral test is used to supplement a written examination.

Who conducts interviews?

The composition of oral boards varies among different jurisdictions. In nearly all, a representative of the personnel department serves as chairman. One of the members of the board may be a representative of the department in which the candidate would work. In some cases, "outside experts" are used, and, frequently, a businessman or some other representative of the general public is asked to serve. Labor and management or other special groups may be represented. The aim is to secure the services of experts in the appropriate field.

However the board is composed, it is a good idea (and not at all improper or unethical) to ascertain in advance of the interview who the members are and what groups they represent. When you are introduced to them, you will have some idea of their backgrounds and interests, and at least you will not stutter and stammer over their names.

What should be done before the interview?

While knowledge about the board members is useful and takes some of the surprise element out of the interview, there is other preparation which is more substantive. It *is* possible to prepare for an oral interview – in several ways:

1) Keep a copy of your application and review it carefully before the interview

This may be the only document before the oral board, and the starting point of the interview. Know what education and experience you have listed there, and the sequence and dates of all of it. Sometimes the board will ask you to review the highlights of your experience for them; you should not have to hem and haw doing it.

2) Study the class specification and the examination announcement

Usually, the oral board has one or both of these to guide them. The qualities, characteristics or knowledges required by the position sought are stated in these documents. They offer valuable clues as to the nature of the oral interview. For example, if the job involves supervisory responsibilities, the announcement will usually indicate that knowledge of modern supervisory methods and the qualifications of the candidate as a supervisor will be tested. If so, you can expect such questions, frequently in the form of a hypothetical situation which you are expected to solve. NEVER go into an oral without knowledge of the duties and responsibilities of the job you seek.

3) Think through each qualification required

Try to visualize the kind of questions you would ask if you were a board member. How well could you answer them? Try especially to appraise your own knowledge and background in each area, *measured against the job sought*, and identify any areas in which you are weak. Be critical and realistic – do not flatter yourself.

4) Do some general reading in areas in which you feel you may be weak

For example, if the job involves supervision and your past experience has NOT, some general reading in supervisory methods and practices, particularly in the field of human relations, might be useful. Do NOT study agency procedures or detailed manuals. The oral board will be testing your understanding and capacity, not your memory.

5) Get a good night's sleep and watch your general health and mental attitude

You will want a clear head at the interview. Take care of a cold or any other minor ailment, and of course, no hangovers.

What should be done on the day of the interview?

Now comes the day of the interview itself. Give yourself plenty of time to get there. Plan to arrive somewhat ahead of the scheduled time, particularly if your appointment is in the fore part of the day. If a previous candidate fails to appear, the board might be ready for you a bit early. By early afternoon an oral board is almost invariably behind schedule if there are many candidates, and you may have to wait. Take along a book or magazine to read, or your application to review, but leave any extraneous material in the waiting room when you go in for your interview. In any event, relax and compose yourself.

The matter of dress is important. The board is forming impressions about you – from your experience, your manners, your attitude, and your appearance. Give your personal appearance careful attention. Dress your best, but not your flashiest. Choose conservative, appropriate clothing, and be sure it is immaculate. This is a business interview, and your appearance should indicate that you regard it as such. Besides, being well groomed and properly dressed will help boost your confidence.

Sooner or later, someone will call your name and escort you into the interview room. *This is it.* From here on you are on your own. It is too late for any more preparation. But remember, you asked for this opportunity to prove your fitness, and you are here because your request was granted.

What happens when you go in?

The usual sequence of events will be as follows: The clerk (who is often the board stenographer) will introduce you to the chairman of the oral board, who will introduce you to the other members of the board. Acknowledge the introductions before you sit down. Do not be surprised if you find a microphone facing you or a stenotypist sitting by. Oral interviews are usually recorded in the event of an appeal or other review.

Usually the chairman of the board will open the interview by reviewing the highlights of your education and work experience from your application – primarily for the benefit of the other members of the board, as well as to get the material into the record. Do not interrupt or comment unless there is an error or significant misinterpretation; if that is the case, do not hesitate. But do not quibble about insignificant matters. Also, he will usually ask you some question about your education, experience or your present job – partly to get you to start talking and to establish the interviewing "rapport." He may start the actual questioning, or turn it over to one of the other members. Frequently, each member undertakes the questioning on a particular area, one in which he is perhaps most competent, so you can expect each member to participate in the examination. Because time is limited, you may also expect some rather abrupt switches in the direction the questioning takes, so do not be upset by it. Normally, a board member will not pursue a single line of questioning unless he discovers a particular strength or weakness.

After each member has participated, the chairman will usually ask whether any member has any further questions, then will ask you if you have anything you wish to add. Unless you are expecting this question, it may floor you. Worse, it may start you off on an extended, extemporaneous speech. The board is not usually seeking more information. The question is principally to offer you a last opportunity to present further qualifications or to indicate that you have nothing to add. So, if you feel that a significant qualification or characteristic has been overlooked, it is proper to point it out in a sentence or so. Do not compliment the board on the thoroughness of their examination – they have been sketchy, and you know it. If you wish, merely say, "No thank you, I have nothing further to add." This is a point where you can "talk yourself out" of a good impression or fail to present an important bit of information. Remember, *you close the interview yourself.*

The chairman will then say, "That is all, Mr. _____, thank you." Do not be startled; the interview is over, and quicker than you think. Thank him, gather your belongings and take your leave. Save your sigh of relief for the other side of the door.

How to put your best foot forward
Throughout this entire process, you may feel that the board individually and collectively is trying to pierce your defenses, seek out your hidden weaknesses and embarrass and confuse you. Actually, this is not true. They are obliged to make an appraisal of your qualifications for the job you are seeking, and they want to see you in your best light. Remember, they must interview all candidates and a non-cooperative candidate may become a failure in spite of their best efforts to bring out his qualifications. Here are 15 suggestions that will help you:

1) Be natural – Keep your attitude confident, not cocky
If you are not confident that you can do the job, do not expect the board to be. Do not apologize for your weaknesses, try to bring out your strong points. The board is interested in a positive, not negative, presentation. Cockiness will antagonize any board member and make him wonder if you are covering up a weakness by a false show of strength.

2) Get comfortable, but don't lounge or sprawl
Sit erectly but not stiffly. A careless posture may lead the board to conclude that you are careless in other things, or at least that you are not impressed by the importance of the occasion. Either conclusion is natural, even if incorrect. Do not fuss with your clothing, a pencil or an ashtray. Your hands may occasionally be useful to emphasize a point; do not let them become a point of distraction.

3) Do not wisecrack or make small talk
This is a serious situation, and your attitude should show that you consider it as such. Further, the time of the board is limited – they do not want to waste it, and neither should you.

4) Do not exaggerate your experience or abilities

In the first place, from information in the application or other interviews and sources, the board may know more about you than you think. Secondly, you probably will not get away with it. An experienced board is rather adept at spotting such a situation, so do not take the chance.

5) If you know a board member, do not make a point of it, yet do not hide it

Certainly you are not fooling him, and probably not the other members of the board. Do not try to take advantage of your acquaintanceship – it will probably do you little good.

6) Do not dominate the interview

Let the board do that. They will give you the clues – do not assume that you have to do all the talking. Realize that the board has a number of questions to ask you, and do not try to take up all the interview time by showing off your extensive knowledge of the answer to the first one.

7) Be attentive

You only have 20 minutes or so, and you should keep your attention at its sharpest throughout. When a member is addressing a problem or question to you, give him your undivided attention. Address your reply principally to him, but do not exclude the other board members.

8) Do not interrupt

A board member may be stating a problem for you to analyze. He will ask you a question when the time comes. Let him state the problem, and wait for the question.

9) Make sure you understand the question

Do not try to answer until you are sure what the question is. If it is not clear, restate it in your own words or ask the board member to clarify it for you. However, do not haggle about minor elements.

10) Reply promptly but not hastily

A common entry on oral board rating sheets is "candidate responded readily," or "candidate hesitated in replies." Respond as promptly and quickly as you can, but do not jump to a hasty, ill-considered answer.

11) Do not be peremptory in your answers

A brief answer is proper – but do not fire your answer back. That is a losing game from your point of view. The board member can probably ask questions much faster than you can answer them.

12) Do not try to create the answer you think the board member wants

He is interested in what kind of mind you have and how it works – not in playing games. Furthermore, he can usually spot this practice and will actually grade you down on it.

13) Do not switch sides in your reply merely to agree with a board member

Frequently, a member will take a contrary position merely to draw you out and to see if you are willing and able to defend your point of view. Do not start a debate, yet do not surrender a good position. If a position is worth taking, it is worth defending.

14) Do not be afraid to admit an error in judgment if you are shown to be wrong

The board knows that you are forced to reply without any opportunity for careful consideration. Your answer may be demonstrably wrong. If so, admit it and get on with the interview.

15) Do not dwell at length on your present job

The opening question may relate to your present assignment. Answer the question but do not go into an extended discussion. You are being examined for a *new* job, not your present one. As a matter of fact, try to phrase ALL your answers in terms of the job for which you are being examined.

Basis of Rating

Probably you will forget most of these "do's" and "don'ts" when you walk into the oral interview room. Even remembering them all will not ensure you a passing grade. Perhaps you did not have the qualifications in the first place. But remembering them will help you to put your best foot forward, without treading on the toes of the board members.

Rumor and popular opinion to the contrary notwithstanding, an oral board wants you to make the best appearance possible. They know you are under pressure – but they also want to see how you respond to it as a guide to what your reaction would be under the pressures of the job you seek. They will be influenced by the degree of poise you display, the personal traits you show and the manner in which you respond.

ABOUT THIS BOOK

This book contains tests divided into Examination Sections. Go through each test, answering every question in the margin. We have also attached a sample answer sheet at the back of the book that can be removed and used. At the end of each test look at the answer key and check your answers. On the ones you got wrong, look at the right answer choice and learn. Do not fill in the answers first. Do not memorize the questions and answers, but understand the answer and principles involved. On your test, the questions will likely be different from the samples. Questions are changed and new ones added. If you understand these past questions you should have success with any changes that arise. Tests may consist of several types of questions. We have additional books on each subject should more study be advisable or necessary for you. Finally, the more you study, the better prepared you will be. This book is intended to be the last thing you study before you walk into the examination room. Prior study of relevant texts is also recommended. NLC publishes some of these in our Fundamental Series. Knowledge and good sense are important factors in passing your exam. Good luck also helps. So now study this Passbook, absorb the material contained within and take that knowledge into the examination. Then do your best to pass that exam.

EXAMINATION SECTION

EXAMINATION SECTION
TEST 1

DIRECTIONS: Each question or incomplete statement is followed by several suggested answers or completions. Select the one that BEST answers the question or completes the statement. *PRINT THE LETTER OF THE CORRECT ANSWER IN THE SPACE AT THE RIGHT.*

1. When instructing elderly patients about home care, which of the following accommodations should be made for patients who suffer from a decreased lens accommodation in their vision?

    A. Repeat the information frequently
    B. Speak slowly
    C. Use an amplifier
    D. Use large illustrations

2. A home health care agency which is owned by an individual or corporation and which provides home care on a for profit basis is called a(n) _____ agency.

    A. voluntary home health   B. proprietary
    C. institution-based   D. governmental

3. A _____ is the person who assists the doctor and registered nurse in performing specialized procedures, and who prepares equipment and helps the patient learn self-care techniques.

    A. licensed practical nurse
    B. medical social worker
    C. home health aide
    D. therapist

4. That proportion of a group or population which develops a disease measured against all of those exposed to a particular risk helps determine the

    A. association   B. causal relationship
    C. incidence rate   D. attack rate

5. The tertiary level of health problem prevention is defined as _____ health problems.

    A. discovery and treatment of existing
    B. reduction of the severity of existing
    C. easing the pain of existing, terminal
    D. prevention of the occurrence of

6. The Rice Model of Dynamic Self-Determination is used to provide a _____-focused model for home health nursing.

    A. nurse   B. patient
    C. caregiver   D. community

7. The comparison of a client's health status with the projected outcomes of care is called

    A. assessment   B. planning
    C. implementation   D. evaluation

8. _____ criteria detects true positives, i.e., a very high percentage of people with the specific disease that was tested for.

   A. Relative risk
   B. Ratio
   C. Specificity
   D. Sensitivity

9. A home health nurse should plan for future visits during which phase of a home health visit?

   A. Initiation
   B. In-home
   C. Termination
   D. Post-visit

10. The secondary level of health problem prevention is defined as _____ health problems.

    A. discovery and treatment of existing
    B. reduction of the severity of existing
    C. easing the pain of existing, terminal
    D. prevention of the occurrence of

11. A patient should be referred to a clinical nurse specialist when

    A. complex patient-care issues are involved
    B. personal care services such as bathing and grooming are required
    C. a patient needs palliative care
    D. a patient has special dietary needs

12. Which of the following are indicators of home-bound status?

    A. Fluctuating blood pressure that results in frequent dizziness
    B. Legal blindness
    C. Dependence on a home ventilator
    D. All of the above

13. The development of goals and objectives is an aspect of the _____ phase of the nursing process.

    A. assessment
    B. planning
    C. implementation
    D. evaluation

14. A count of all the people suffering from a particular health condition which exists in a given population at a particular time establishes the

    A. prevalence of the condition
    B. incidence of the condition
    C. relative risk to other individuals
    D. specificity of the condition

15. During a home visit, how should the home nurse wash his/her hands?

    A. With sterile cloths from the nurse's bag
    B. At a sink with warm running water, soap, and paper towels
    C. The home nurse should wear sterile gloves at all times
    D. Using water that has been boiled and allowed to cool, and sterile cloths

16. During which stage of the home health care process does the nurse record the client's health status, nursing interventions employed, and the effectiveness of those interventions?

    A. Assessment
    B. Planning
    C. Implementation
    D. Evaluation

17. The nursing bag should be treated as a(n) _____ during a home health visit.

    A. instructive tool to be shared with the patient
    B. defensive instrument, if necessary
    C. clean area
    D. contaminated area

18. The Omaha Visiting Nurse Association System is an attempt to

    A. adopt a professional code of behavior and dress for nurses and nurse practitioners
    B. adopt standardized nursing diagnoses
    C. adapt standardized nursing diagnoses to individual health situations
    D. adapt standardized nursing diagnoses to community health situations

19. Home services for terminally ill patients are provided by _____ agencies.

    A. hospice
    B. proprietary
    C. institution-based
    D. governmental

20. Statements of behaviors expected of the nurse in carrying out a plan of care are called

    A. objectives
    B. process objectives
    C. outcome objectives
    D. goals

21. The post-visit phase of a home visit is primarily used for which of the following purposes?

    A. Clarifying the need for the home visit
    B. Establishing the nurse-client relationship
    C. Reviewing the visit with a patient's family members
    D. Recording the visit and planning for the next visit

22. When the disease rate exceeds normal or expected frequency in a particular community or region, it is considered a(n)

    A. epidemic
    B. pandemic
    C. outbreak
    D. relative risk

23. Chewing calamus root is sometimes used as a home remedy for

    A. diarrhea
    B. constipation
    C. upset stomach
    D. sore throat

24. Increased exercise and fitness is an example of

    A. health promotion
    B. health prevention
    C. health protection
    D. secondary prevention

25. When a patient is suffering from impaired balance and/or coordination, which of the following home nurse referrals would be most appropriate? 25.____

    A. Psychiatric
    B. Skilled
    C. Occupational therapy
    D. Physical therapy

KEY (CORRECT ANSWERS)

1.	D	11.	A
2.	B	12.	D
3.	A	13.	B
4.	D	14.	A
5.	B	15.	B
6.	B	16.	D
7.	C	17.	C
8.	D	18.	D
9.	C	19.	A
10.	A	20.	B

21. D
22. A
23. C
24. A
25. D

TEST 2

DIRECTIONS: Each question or incomplete statement is followed by several suggested answers or completions. Select the one that BEST answers the question or completes the statement. *PRINT THE LETTER OF THE CORRECT ANSWER IN THE SPACE AT THE RIGHT.*

1. To provide barrier protection against infectious droplet agents, the home health nurse should use a

    A. mask or respiratory device
    B. private room
    C. private room with negative airflow and a mask
    D. private room with negative airflow

2. To drain the right middle lobe of a patient's lung using chest wall percussion and vibration, the patient should be lying on his

    A. right side, with his feet elevated
    B. left side, with his feet elevated
    C. back, with his feet elevated
    D. left side, with his right side supported and his feet elevated

3. When working with mental health patients, which of the following teaching strategies should be used?

    A. Instruct with simplified teaching tools, such as models and illustrations
    B. Focus on building trust and acceptance, and avoid confrontation
    C. Speak slowly and loudly
    D. Repeat information frequently and use analogies

4. Data collection and analysis are aspects of what phase of the nursing process?

    A. Assessment
    B. Planning
    C. Implementation
    D. Evaluation

5. An organization which is primarily engaged in providing skilled nursing services and other therapeutic services to patients in their homes is called a _____ health agency.

    A. voluntary nonprofit
    B. public nonprofit
    C. proprietary home
    D. home

6. Assessment of the outcome of nursing intervention is called

    A. assessment
    B. planning evaluation
    C. process evaluation
    D. outcome evaluation

7. What are the elements of malpractice, in their proper order?

    A. Causation, duty, breach of duty, injury
    B. Duty, injury, and causation
    C. Duty, breach of duty, injury, and causation
    D. Breach of duty, injury, and causation

1._____
2._____
3._____
4._____
5._____
6._____
7._____

8. Broad statements of outcome in the planning phase of nursing intervention are referred to as

   A. process objectives
   B. goals
   C. outcome objectives
   D. objectives

9. A process whose goal is to eliminate the overuse of health care services in order to decrease payments for those services is called _____ review.

   A. utilization
   B. retrospective
   C. quality assurance
   D. criteria

10. What do plague, rabies, gonorrhea, and rubella have in common?

    A. They are all notifiable.
    B. They are all curable.
    C. None of them is curable, but all are treatable.
    D. They primarily affect the poor and uneducated.

11. When should Intermittent Positive Pressure Breathing (IPPB) treatments be administered?

    A. When patients are susceptible to pneumothorax
    B. When the patient can sit upright without assistance
    C. Before meals
    D. After meals

12. Predetermined indicators which help measure whether a standard care has been met are called

    A. audits
    B. health standards
    C. care standards
    D. criteria

13. How should the home health nurse dispose of soiled dressings in the patient's home?

    A. Simply place dressings in the patient's outdoor garbage bin
    B. Disinfect with a bleach solution if possible and then place in an empty, sealed plastic bag for disposal in the patient's home
    C. Disinfect with a bleach solution if possible and then place in an empty, sealed plastic bag for disposal at the home health agency
    D. The dressings should be burned

14. How should a mistaken entry in a medical record be corrected?

    A. Erase the mistaken information and rewrite
    B. Begin a new report
    C. Report the mistake immediately to your supervisor
    D. Draw a line through the mistaken information, and then initial and date the entry

15. Groups like Alcoholics Anonymous are examples of which type of health problem prevention?

    A. Primary
    B. Secondary
    C. Tertiary
    D. Protective

16. The physical design of a home is a factor in which type of assessment?

    A. Environmental B. Cultural
    C. Adult   D. Situational

17. A home health care agency which is publicly funded is called a(n) _____ agency.

    A. voluntary home health B. proprietary
    C. institution-based   D. governmental

18. Castor oil is sometimes used as a home remedy for

    A. diarrhea B. constipation
    C. cough   D. fever

19. Which of the following is an example of objective documentation?

    A. Patient's color is good.
    B. Patient appears depressed.
    C. Patient is learning how to care for wound.
    D. Right foot and toes cool to touch. Patient complains of tingling sensation in toes.

20. Which type of data is observed directly by the nurse?

    A. Objective B. Subjective
    C. Tertiary   D. Secondary

21. Place 30 ml of bleach into a sterile jar. Add sterile water until jar is filled. Cover with a sterile lid and store at room temperature.
    The above procedure describes the process for making which of the following?

    A. Normal saline
    B. Acetic acid
    C. Modified Dakin's solution
    D. Chloramine T

22. A statement of expected changes in client's health is called a(n)

    A. objective   B. process objective
    C. outcome objective D. goal

23. An investigation whose goal is to identify associations to a particular disease and its possible cause is called a(n) _____ study.

    A. analytic   B. descriptive
    C. experimental   D. retrospective

24. A cabbage leaf poultice is sometimes used as a home remedy for

    A. earache B. toothache
    C. cough   D. fever

25. A description of those people considered disease cases, where no comparison group is present and no conclusions can be drawn, is called a(n)

    A. cohort group B. association group
    C. case series   D. population at risk

KEY (CORRECT ANSWERS)

1.	C	11.	C
2.	D	12.	D
3.	B	13.	B
4.	A	14.	D
5.	D	15.	C
6.	D	16.	A
7.	C	17.	D
8.	B	18.	B
9.	A	19.	D
10.	A	20.	A

21. C
22. C
23. A
24. D
25. C

TEST 3

DIRECTIONS: Each question or incomplete statement is followed by several suggested answers or completions. Select the one that BEST answers the question or completes the statement. *PRINT THE LETTER OF THE CORRECT ANSWER IN THE SPACE AT THE RIGHT.*

1. The proper home cleaning procedure for nasal cannules, masks, tubing, and humidifiers is

    A. washing them in soap and water
    B. washing them in soap and water, and then soaking in a bleach solution
    C. immersion in a bleach solution for twenty minutes
    D. immersion in boiling water for twenty minutes

2. A home health nurse should review referral and family records during the _____ phase of a home health visit.

    A. initiation   B. previsit
    C. in-home   D. post-visit

3. Comparing the occurrence of a disease in a group of people when a particular factor is present to a group of people when that factor is not present establishes the

    A. relative risk   B. incidence rate
    C. prevalence rate   D. morbidity

4. A patient who requires joint protection techniques and pain control should receive which of the following home nurse referrals?

    A. Psychiatric   B. Skilled
    C. Occupational therapy   D. Physical therapy

5. When instructing elderly patients about home care, which of the following accommodations should be made for patients who require a longer reaction time?

    A. Repeat the information frequently, and use videos and practice to reinforce the concepts
    B. Speak slowly, and ask the patient to use a hearing aid
    C. Use an amplifier, along with a magnifying mirror
    D. Use large illustrations, and teach only one concept at a time

6. The person who makes the initial home evaluation visit, initiates the treatment plan, provides those services which requires specialized nursing skill, prepares appropriate notes and coordinates services is the

    A. registered nurse   B. licensed practical nurse
    C. medical social worker   D. doctor

7. A(n) _____ relationship can be inferred if the incidence rate of disease increases when the putative cause is present and decreases when it is absent.

    A. associated   B. causal
    C. morbid   D. epidemic

8. Consideration of a patient's independence and ability to perform basic activities for daily living is used in what type of assessment?

    A. Environmental
    B. Child-bearing
    C. Situational
    D. Cultural

9. Stated goals for health care activities that can be used to plan and evaluate care are called

    A. criteria
    B. quality assurances
    C. audits
    D. standards of care

10. Which of the following is considered a minor abnormality in a newborn baby?

    A. An inability to see the tympanic membrane because of filled aural canal
    B. The low placement of ears
    C. The absence of reflex in response to loud noise
    D. Nonpatent nose canals

11. A home health nurse should schedule a home visit during which phase of a home health visit?

    A. Initiation
    B. Previsit
    C. In-home
    D. Termination

12. Drinking blackberry juice is sometimes used as a home remedy for

    A. diarrhea
    B. constipation
    C. cold
    D. upset stomach

13. An investigation that describes groups of people in terms of certain characteristics as they relate to disease occurrence is called a(n) _____ study.

    A. analytic
    B. retrospective
    C. descriptive
    D. prospective

14. A patient should be referred to a home health aide when

    A. complex patient-care issues are involved
    B. personal care services such as bathing and grooming are required
    C. a patient needs palliative care
    D. a patient has special dietary needs

15. The primary level of health problem prevention is defined as _____ health problems.

    A. discovery and treatment of existing
    B. reduction of the severity of existing
    C. easing the pain of existing, terminal
    D. prevention of the occurrence of

16. To provide barrier protection against infectious airborne agents, the home health nurse should use a

    A. mask or respiratory device
    B. private room
    C. private room with negative airflow and gloves
    D. private room with negative airflow and a mask or respiratory device

17. Wounds with necrotic debris can be treated with

   A. Dakin's
   B. betadine
   C. hydrogen peroxide
   D. isopropyl alcohol

18. Boil 6 cups of tap water for 20 minutes, then allow to cool. Pour 4 cups of boiled water into a clean jar and add 2 teaspoons of salt. Mix well. Place lid on the jar and store in the refrigerator.
   The above procedure describes the process for making which of the following?

   A. Normal saline
   B. A sterile jar
   C. Modified Dakin's solution
   D. Chloramine T

19. A group of people who share a common experience during a specified period of time are considered

   A. agents
   B. cohorts
   C. hosts
   D. a case series

20. A patient who is suffering from a terminal condition, but who does not receive care from hospice, should receive which of the following home nurse referrals?

   A. Psychiatric
   B. Skilled
   C. Occupational therapy
   D. Social service

21. A process of quality assessment that examines patterns of care over a limited period of time in the past is called a(n)

   A. retrospective review
   B. concurrent review
   C. peer review
   D. audit

22. Which of the following is an example of effective dry-heat sterilization?

   A. Place dressings in boiling water for 1 hour
   B. Wrap dressings in a clean cloth and place in direct sunlight for 2 hours
   C. Wrap dressings in a clean cloth and place in a metal pan in a 350 degree oven for 1 hour
   D. Run dressings through the hot cycle of a dishwasher

23. The person who reviews and directs the treatment plan is the

   A. registered nurse
   B. licensed practical nurse
   C. medical social worker
   D. doctor

24. The premise that a home health organization performs many activities that contribute to the assurance of quality care, and that these activities must be organized so that they include all the important program components is referred to as a

   A. utilization review package
   B. standards of care package
   C. quality assurance package
   D. criteria program

25. As an element of malpractice, duty is established or created by
    A. a professional relationship
    B. a legal relationship
    C. an ethical relationship
    D. all of the above

KEY (CORRECT ANSWERS)

1.	A	11.	B
2.	B	12.	A
3.	A	13.	C
4.	C	14.	B
5.	A	15.	D
6.	A	16.	D
7.	B	17.	C
8.	C	18.	A
9.	D	19.	B
10.	A	20.	D

21. A
22. C
23. D
24. C
25. A

EXAMINATION SECTION
TEST 1

DIRECTIONS: Each question or incomplete statement is followed by several suggested answers or completions. Select the one that BEST answers the question or completes the statement. *PRINT THE LETTER OF THE CORRECT ANSWER IN THE SPACE AT THE RIGHT.*

1. What is the difference between the objective documentation of a patient's condition and subjective documentation?

    A. Objective documentation focuses on a doctor's conclusions, while subjective documentation focuses on a nurse's conclusions.
    B. Objective documentation focuses on a nurse's conclusions, while subjective documentation focuses on a doctor's conclusions.
    C. Objective documentation focuses on the facts, while subjective documentation focuses on a nurse's conclusions without providing supporting facts.
    D. Subjective documentation focuses on the facts, while objective documentation focuses on a nurse's conclusions without providing supporting facts.

1.____

2. The fluoridation of community water supplies is an example of which of the following?

    A. Secondary prevention
    B. Health prevention
    C. Health promotion
    D. Health protection

2.____

3. Which of the following types of tea is sometimes used as a home remedy for the common cold?

    A. Ginger
    B. Comfrey
    C. Cinammon
    D. Jerusalem Oak

3.____

4. While off-duty, a home health nurse comes across a man lying on the sidewalk outside of her bank. The home health nurse is recognized by one of the bystanders as a caregiver, and asked to assist.
   Which of the following best describes the nature of the nurse's responsibility in this situation?
   The nurse has

    A. both an ethical and a legal responsibility to help the man
    B. an ethical responsibility to help, but no legal responsibility
    C. a legal responsibility to help the man, but no ethical responsibility
    D. both an ethical and a legal responsibility, and she is also liable for any injuries the man might sustain as a result of her intervention

4.____

5. Chest wall percussion and vibration techniques are used to

    A. resuscitate heartbeat function
    B. resuscitate breathing function
    C. remove secretions from the lungs
    D. check for pulmonary blockage

5.____

6. A soap-rinse decreases the effectiveness of which of the following wound treatments?

    A. Hibiclens
    B. Isopropyl
    C. Acetic acid
    D. Hydrogen peroxide

6.____

13

7. Which of the following can be used as a disinfectant during a home care visit? 7.____

   A. Bleach   B. Diluted bleach
   C. White vinegar   D. All of the above

8. A breast self-examination is an example of which type of health problem prevention? 8.____

   A. Primary   B. Secondary
   C. Tertiary   D. Protective

9. Specific achievements which are expected to result in goal outcomes are called 9.____

   A. objectives   B. process objectives
   C. outcome objectives   D. goals

10. As a home health nurse, if you are assigned a case which requires skills beyond your qualifications or abilities, you should 10.____

    A. attempt to learn the skills that will be required of you as quickly as possible
    B. refuse the assignment
    C. accept the decision of your superior and take the case
    D. notify the patient of your lack of qualifications

11. When working with pediatric patients, which of the following teaching strategies should be used? 11.____

    A. Speak slowly and loudly
    B. Allow children to focus on other activities while you're speaking, such as coloring or playing
    C. Instruct with demonstration models, such as dolls or stuffed animals
    D. Provide only small amounts of information at each session

12. A process which assesses the quality of care while the care is being given is called 12.____

    A. auditing   B. quality assurance
    C. retrospective review   D. concurrent review

13. The ratio of sick individuals to the total population of a community is called 13.____

    A. the population at risk   B. the incidence rate
    C. morbidity   D. the mortality rate

14. A home health nurse should clarify the purpose for the home visit during which of the following phases? 14.____

    A. Initiation   B. Previsit
    C. In-home   D. Termination

15. What is the primary danger associated with administering oxygen to patients in their homes? 15.____

    A. Overdose danger to patient
    B. Combustibility
    C. Overdose danger to children
    D. Leaking or spillage

16. Mix sterile water and a chlorazine tablet together in a small, clean container describes the process for making 16.____

    A. normal saline
    B. acetic acid
    C. modified Dakin's solution
    D. Chloramine T

17. When events appear together more often than they would by chance alone, they are considered 17.____

    A. causally associated B. pandemic
    C. associated D. endemic

18. To drain the base of the patient's left lung using chest wall percussion and vibration, the patient should be lying on his 18.____

    A. right side, with his feet elevated by 50 cm
    B. left side, with his feet elevated by 50 cm
    C. back, with his feet elevated 50 cm
    D. right side, with his left side supported, and his feet level with his body

19. Home health visits are designed to meet which of the following goals? 19.____

    A. Case finding/referral B. Health promotion
    C. Care of the sick D. All of the above

20. MIST stands for 20.____

    A. Mother Infant Standardization Test
    B. Maternal Instinct Screening Tool
    C. Mother Infant Screening Tool
    D. Maternal Instinct Standardization Test

21. A notation of contact with a patient, which is written and dated by a member of the health team, and which describes symptoms, treatment and drugs administered is called 21.____

    A. progress note B. clinical note
    C. summary report D. subunit

22. An organized effort on the part of professionals to monitor and assess the quality and appropriateness of nursing care provided by peers in relation to professional standards of conduct is called 22.____

    A. audit B. concurrent review
    C. peer review D. criteria review

23. What should the home health nurse do if a relative or neighbor of the patient presents a safety threat to the nurse? 23.____

    A. Arrange joint visits with another home health nurse
    B. Schedule an appointment time when the relative or neighbor can not be present
    C. Terminate all visits if the safety problem is not resolved
    D. All of the above

24. Under what circumstances can a late entry about a home health visit be made?

    A. When a mistake was made during the visit which might result in malpractice liability
    B. When a mistake was made in the initial entry
    C. When no entry was made
    D. All of the above

25. A home health care agency which provides home health visits on a nonprofit basis is termed a _____ agency.

    A. voluntary home health
    B. proprietary
    C. institution-based
    D. governmental

KEY (CORRECT ANSWERS)

1. C		11. C
2. D		12. D
3. A		13. C
4. B		14. A
5. C		15. B
6. A		16. D
7. D		17. C
8. B		18. A
9. A		19. D
10. B		20. C

21. B
22. A
23. D
24. C
25. A

TEST 2

DIRECTIONS: Each question or incomplete statement is followed by several suggested answers or completions. Select the one that BEST answers the question or completes the statement. *PRINT THE LETTER OF THE CORRECT ANSWER IN THE SPACE AT THE RIGHT.*

1. The PROCESS recording form is used for

    A. environmental assessment for adults
    B. cultural assessment for adults
    C. environmental assessment for children
    D. cultural assessment for children

2. Organizations of doctors who monitor the need, appropriateness, and quality of health services financed by federal dollars are called

    A. professional review organizations
    B. peer review committees
    C. quality assurance committees
    D. concurrent review committees

3. Scaling cues of no competence, moderate competence, and complete competence are levels of

    A. cultural assessment
    B. environmental assessment
    C. situational assessment
    D. family coping index

4. Living wills, DNR orders, and the appointment of health care agents are all examples of

    A. proxy directives
    B. advance directives
    C. patient responsibilities
    D. patient rights

5. The primary, secondary, and tertiary levels of preventive action are elements of which stage of the nursing process?

    A. Assessment
    B. Planning
    C. Intervention
    D. Evaluation

6. When a patient is suffering from high anxiety and/or unrelieved stress, which of the following home nurse referrals would be most appropriate?

    A. Psychiatric
    B. Skilled
    C. Occupational therapy
    D. Physical therapy

7. The organization and carrying-out of the plan of care is referred to as

    A. assessment
    B. evaluation
    C. implementation
    D. nursing intervention

8. What are the steps of the nursing process, in their proper order?

    A. Planning, assessment, implementation, and evaluation
    B. Planning, implementation, assessment, and evaluation
    C. Evaluation, planning, implementation, and assessment
    D. Assessment, planning, implementation, and evaluation

9. Which of the following is an advantage of home nursing?

   A. Achieving a balance between intimacy and distance
   B. Access
   C. Safety
   D. Achieving a balance between dependence and independence

10. To provide barrier protection against infectious contact agents, the home health nurse should use a

    A. mask or respiratory device
    B. private room
    C. private room with negative airflow, gloves, and a gown
    D. private room with negative airflow and a mask or respiratory device

11. Examination of the quality of actions taken and the processes used to achieve specific outcomes is referred to as

    A. assessment   B. planning evaluation
    C. process evaluation D. outcome evaluation

12. Family planning is an example of which of the following types of community health services?

    A. Tertiary   B. Preventive
    C. Health protection   D. Health promotion

13. Good Samaritan laws provide immunity for

    A. flight from the scene of an injury
    B. abstention (the decision to NOT provide aid or assistance to an injured person)
    C. gross negligence
    D. negligence

14. Services provided by an individual who has assumed care responsibility for a homebound person on a temporary basis are called _____ care services.

    A. hospice   B. intermittent
    C. respite   D. institution-based

15. When making family assessments, which of the following factors should the community health nurse consider before intervening?

    A. Cultural factors   B. Socioeconomic factors
    C. Racial factors   D. All of the above

16. When instructing elderly patients about home care, which of the following accommodations should be made for patients who suffer from decreased short term memory?

    A. Slow the pace of the presentation and use analogies
    B. Teach one concept at a time, and use oral and written demonstration to reinforce concepts
    C. Use an amplifier and a magnifying mirror, if possible
    D. Use large illustrations and make sure eyeglasses are worn

17. Which of the following can be made in a patient's home?

    A. Cartridge inhalers
    B. Compression nebulizers
    C. Hydrogen peroxide
    D. Sterile normal saline

18. A patient should be referred to a hospice when

    A. complex patient-care issues are involved
    B. personal care services such as bathing and grooming are required
    C. a patient needs palliative care
    D. a patient has special dietary needs

19. Iodine sensitive wounds should be treated with

    A. Dakin's
    B. alcohol/ethanol
    C. hydrogen peroxide
    D. betadine

20. A home health care agency which provides home care as part of a larger institution is called a(n) _____ agency.

    A. voluntary home health
    B. proprietary
    C. institution-based
    D. governmental

21. A method for recording client data, intended outcomes, plans for achieving those outcomes, and which also reflects both positive and negative client health status is called a _____ record.

    A. nursing
    B. patient-oriented
    C. problem-oriented
    D. status-oriented

22. Which of the following is a challenge in home nursing care?

    A. Access
    B. Safety
    C. Family and cultural information
    D. All of the above

23. A case manager's responsibilities include

    A. maintenance of standards of care, coordination of services, and supervision of patient/caregiver outcomes
    B. maintenance of his/her patients' care, including the performance of all necessary medical procedures
    C. coordination of patient's family care schedule, as well as supervision of all payment and billing information
    D. maintenance of all billing records and payments received

24. An immunization shot is an example of _____ health problem prevention.

    A. primary
    B. secondary
    C. tertiary
    D. protective

25. Therapeutic competence is a factor in _____ assessment.

    A. community
    B. environmental
    C. situational
    D. family

KEY (CORRECT ANSWERS)

1.	C	11.	C
2.	A	12.	B
3.	D	13.	D
4.	B	14.	C
5.	B	15.	A
6.	A	16.	B
7.	C	17.	D
8.	D	18.	C
9.	B	19.	B
10.	C	20.	C

21. D
22. B
23. A
24. A
25. D

TEST 3

DIRECTIONS: Each question or incomplete statement is followed by several suggested answers or completions. Select the one that BEST answers the question or completes the statement. *PRINT THE LETTER OF THE CORRECT ANSWER IN THE SPACE AT THE RIGHT.*

1. Which type of data is provided by the client or patient?   1.____

   A. Objective
   B. Subjective
   C. Both objective and subjective
   D. Tertiary

2. A tobacco poultice is sometimes used as a home remedy for   2.____

   A. earaches   B. fever   C. boils   D. splinters

3. The basic working unit of a quality assurance program is the   3.____

   A. peer review committee
   B. professional review organization
   C. criteria committee
   D. concurrent review committee

4. Fill a small-mouth jar with tap water. Stand jar upright in a pot, and fill the pot so that water covers the jar. Drop jar lid into pot, and cover pot. Boil for at least 20 minutes. Use sterile tongs to remove jar from pot. Remove jar lid from pot with sterile tongs and place on jar (touching only the outside of the jar lid).   4.____
   The above procedure describes the process for making which of the following?

   A. Normal saline
   B. A sterile jar
   C. Modified Dakin's solution
   D. Chloramine T

5. The process which involves the comparison of a health-care situation against accepted standards of quality care, the identification of care strengths and weaknesses, and the introduction of changes into the health-care process is called   5.____

   A. peer review   B. concurrent review
   C. criteria review   D. quality assurance

6. Epidemics that are worldwide in distribution are considered   6.____

   A. endemic   B. pandemic   C. epidemic   D. prevalent

7. The person assigned to a particular patient by a registered nurse, and whose responsibilities include carrying out the health-care plan designed by the registered nurse, including the taking of body temperature, pulse, and respiration is the   7.____

   A. medical social worker   B. therapist
   C. home health worker   D. physician's assistant

8. The formation of a hypothesis is an aspect of the _____ phase of the nursing process.   8.____

   A. assessment   B. planning
   C. implementation   D. evaluation

9. During a home visit, the nurse should place his/her bag on paper bags or newspaper in order to prevent _____ contamination.

   A. nurse to client
   B. client to nurse
   C. client to client
   D. all of the above

10. When working with illiterate patients, which of the following teaching strategies should be used?

    A. Instruct with simplified teaching tools, such as models and illustrations
    B. Speak slowly and loudly
    C. Use an amplifier and a magnifying mirror
    D. Repeat information frequently and use analogies

11. Documentation of a home visit should include which of the following types of information?

    A. Presence of a private sitter or companion
    B. Fractures or disabilities that prevent ambulation without the assistance of aids
    C. Medications reviewed with the client
    D. All of the above

12. In an environment which presents a reasonable likelihood of exposure to blood or body substances, which of the following activities should be avoided by the home health nurse?

    A. Eating and drinking
    B. Washing hands in patient's sink
    C. Use of any sharp instruments
    D. Collection of specimens

13. People who share one or more characteristics and who could have suffered from a particular disease whether or not they actually did, are considered to be

    A. prospective hosts
    B. a population at risk
    C. sensitive
    D. agents

14. A patient should be referred to a nutritional specialist when

    A. complex patient-care issues are involved
    B. personal care services such as bathing and grooming are required
    C. a patient needs palliative care
    D. a patient has special dietary needs

15. A statement which provides evidence of need for home health services which are not being met by existing agencies is called a

    A. financial statement
    B. medical release
    C. certificate of need
    D. liability release

16. Designating responsibility for the implementation and delegation of care are aspects of which stage of the nursing process?

    A. Assessment
    B. Planning
    C. Implementation
    D. Evaluation

17. When instructing elderly patients about home care, which of the following accommodations should be made for patients who suffer from an inability to make strong distinctions between sounds?

    A. Repeat the information frequently, and use videos and practice to reinforce the concepts
    B. Speak slowly and eliminate background noise
    C. Use a magnifying mirror and avoid blue or green paper
    D. Use large illustrations and shout if necessary

18. Boil 6 cups of water in a pan for 20 minutes, and allow to cool. Add to a clean jar, along with 4 tablespoons of white distilled vinegar. Mix well.
The above procedure describes the process for making which of the following?

    A. Normal saline
    B. Acetic acid
    C. Modified Dakin's solution
    D. Chloramine T

19. When a patient requires tube feedings, catheter care, and tracheostomy aspiration, which of the following home nurse referrals would be most appropriate?

    A. Psychiatric   B. Skilled
    C. Occupational therapy   D. Physical therapy

20. A patient's attitudes about ethnic groups, young people, elderly people, and women and men are examples of _____ factors in _____ assessment.

    A. environmental; community
    B. socio-cultural; community
    C. diagnostic; senility
    D. diagnostic; physical

21. Specific statements of actions to be taken in order to achieve stated objectives are called

    A. objectives   B. process objectives
    C. outcome objectives   D. nursing interventions

22. The presence of _____ increases the likelihood that a disease will occur in a particular person.

    A. risk factor   B. sensitivity
    C. morbidity   D. relative risk

23. What should the home health nurse do with her purse (which contains personal belongings such as a wallet and checkbook) while she is in the patient's house?

    A. Keep it with her medical bag and supplies
    B. Keep it on her person at all times
    C. She should not bring her purse into the house
    D. Set it down in a safe place until she leaves

24. Which of the following is an example of subjective documentation?   24.____

    A. Left hand pink and warm to the touch
    B. Skin color good
    C. Client able to clean and dress wound
    D. Weight is down by 2 pounds

25. Molasses is sometimes used as a topical home remedy for   25.____

    A. toothache   B. boils
    C. chest cold   D. earache

KEY (CORRECT ANSWERS)

1.	B	11.	B
2.	C	12.	A
3.	A	13.	B
4.	B	14.	D
5.	D	15.	C
6.	B	16.	C
7.	C	17.	B
8.	A	18.	B
9.	D	19.	B
10.	A	20.	B

21. D
22. A
23. C
24. B
25. D

EXAMINATION SECTION
TEST 1

DIRECTIONS: Each question or incomplete statement is followed by several suggested answers or completions. Select the one that BEST answers the question or completes the statement. *PRINT THE LETTER OF THE CORRECT ANSWER IN THE SPACE AT THE RIGHT.*

1. Which of the following is the most probable explanation for vitamin A deficiency in children?

    A. Their unwillingness to eat vegetables
    B. Inadequate vitamin A intake by women during pregnancy
    C. Increased requirements for growth
    D. Inadequate bone development

2. The first step in re-integrating an ill person into the family home would be to

    A. inspect the physical environment in the home
    B. identify family resources and deficits
    C. identify the client's most urgent needs
    D. instruct the family members about home care of the client

3. Which of the following statements about cow's milk is FALSE?

    A. If it is used for infant feeding, it should be pasteurized.
    B. If it is boiled, it is more easily digestible for an infant than milk that is pasteurized.
    C. It does not need to be boiled before being fed to infants.
    D. It must be boiled over a direct flame for 2-3 minutes in order to be considered safe.

4. The overall function of a local department of health is to

    A. protect the health of the people under its jurisdiction
    B. prevent the spread of disease
    C. provide a medical and nursing staff for case investigation
    D. provide an adequate immunization program

5. A family who cans many fruits and vegetables can be taught that a good way of retaining nearly all of the vitamin C content of these canned vegetables is to

    A. vacuum-pack them
    B. quick-freeze them
    C. strain them into a paste
    D. quickly bring them to a boil before freezing

6. A nurse is engaged in an assessment of this client's ability to achieve wellness, applying Pender's model of health promotion.
A modifying factor involved in the client's ability to participate in health-promoting behavior is the

    A. influence of the client's family
    B. client's perceived level of control over his or her health
    C. barriers which the client perceives to be health-promoting behavior
    D. overall importance of health to the client

7. Erickson's theory of psychosocial development states that from ages one to three, the toddler's primary task is to develop

   A. trust B. ingenuity C. autonomy D. self-concept

8. The *bacteriological era* in public health began with the work of

   A. Salk B. Roentgen C. Lister D. Pasteur

9. A low-income family produces and cans much of its own food. In teaching members of this family about food preservation, the nurse should tell them that each of the following is a method for preserving food EXCEPT

   A. using sodium silicate
   B. using benzoate of soda
   C. drying
   D. dehydration

10. Piaget's theory of cognitive development is useful to nurses in health promotion in that it assists nurses in

    A. understanding how children of various ages view and interpret health care measures
    B. identifying the basic physical and psychosocial needs of children
    C. providing a basis for the assessment of a child's moral code
    D. providing the client with tools to conquer personality crises

11. For most children, proteins should form about _____ % of the total daily calorie intake.

    A. 5 B. 15 C. 35 D. 50

12. A client, a student in her 20s, is admitted to the hospital after suffering a back injury in a boating accident. She is on bed rest, in pelvic traction, and may require surgery. The client is worried she may miss the fall semester of university classes if she undergoes surgery. A nurse applying Sister Callista Roy's adaptation model of nursing care would begin planning care for this client by

    A. entering into a caring relationship with the client
    B. identifying how the client's current situation is limiting her ability for self-care
    C. determining whether the accident has damaged the client's sense of self-worth
    D. assessing the stressors acting upon the client

13. Among Americans of _____ descent, sickle-cell disease during pregnancy is most likely to occur.

    A. Native American
    B. African
    C. Oriental Asian
    D. Italian or Greek

14. When preparing a client for a series of diagnostic tests, a nurse should

    A. provide only the amount of information with which the client appears to be able to cope
    B. provide detailed information about each test involved in the series
    C. wait until just prior to the test in order to postpone unnecessary anxiety
    D. provide minimal answers to client questions if the client appears anxious

15. Families who cannot afford refrigeration are at risk primarily because

    A. their food will look and smell unnatural
    B. the activity of enzymes and microorganisms in food will not be retarded
    C. their food will not be sterilized
    D. decomposition will become too apparent to be appetizing

16. The primary focus of the adaptive health model is

    A. stability   B. growth   C. maturity   D. change

17. Which of the following teaching methods or practices is most appropriate for elderly clients?

    A. Encouraging participation in the teaching plan by setting mutual goals
    B. Helping the client learn about feelings and the need for self-expression
    C. Using simple words to promote understanding
    D. Keeping teaching sessions short

18. When conducting a community assessment, a nurse should consider each of the following to be *core* elements of the community EXCEPT

    A. vital statistics
    B. physical environment
    C. values, beliefs, or religion
    D. racial distribution

19. Prolonged labor is most likely to increase the risk of _____ in the newborn.

    A. hyaline membrane disease
    B. Rh disease
    C. cleft palate
    D. intracranial hemorrhage

20. A person's illness may typically affect his/her family in each of the following ways EXCEPT

    A. decreasing interaction
    B. forcing role changes
    C. creating changes in social customs
    D. causing financial problems

21. Patient and family education in home care for peripheral vascular disease would typically include the teaching of each of the following EXCEPT the

    A. practice of changing socks daily
    B. practice of trimming toenails once a week
    C. need to keep feet warm
    D. need to keep feet clean and dry

22. Which of the following is the best explanation for the relatively higher incidence of obesity in low-income communities?

    A. Food preferences of cultural or ethnic groups who predominate these populations
    B. A tendency to purchase greater amounts of pre-processed foods
    C. A greater reliance on dairy products
    D. A reliance on cheaper cuts of meat

23. A client would be described as experiencing Selye's local adaptation syndrome (LAS) if she presents the symptom of

    A. headache
    B. fatigue
    C. hypertension
    D. inflammation

24. Which of the following groups is LEAST likely to experience premature birth?

    A. Mothers who smoke
    B. Mothers who have plural births
    C. Mothers younger than 16
    D. Multigravidas older than 40

25. When planning nutritional counseling for a client, each of the following is an important consideration EXCEPT

    A. cultural acceptability
    B. foods containing the greatest amount of nutrients
    C. prevalence
    D. economic availability

KEY (CORRECT ANSWERS)

1. A		11. B	
2. B		12. D	
3. C		13. B	
4. A		14. A	
5. B		15. B	
6. A		16. A	
7. C		17. D	
8. D		18. B	
9. A		19. D	
10. A		20. A	

21. C
22. B
23. D
24. D
25. C

TEST 2

DIRECTIONS: Each question or incomplete statement is followed by several suggested answers or completions. Select the one that BEST answers the question or completes the statement. *PRINT THE LETTER OF THE CORRECT ANSWER IN THE SPACE AT THE RIGHT.*

1. The hearing of all school-aged children should be checked by means of a screening test at least once every

    A. three months
    B. six months
    C. one year
    D. two years

2. An example of an external variable that exerts a negative influence over a person's health beliefs or practices is the client's

    A. levels of growth and development appear to be retarded
    B. limited knowledge about body functions and illnesses
    C. coming from a family that avoids doctors whenever possible
    D. failure to exercise

3. For many reasons, conventional family planning programs do not always result in preventing pregnancies among adolescents. Which of the following is probably NOT one of these reasons?

    A. Taking contraceptives constitutes the admission of the intent to have sexual relations.
    B. Teenagers are generally more sexually active than more mature adults.
    C. Teenagers do not always expect to become sexually involved with other teens.
    D. Contraceptives are often not made available to sexually active teenagers.

4. A person who believes that good health may be the result of good luck or a reward from God for good behavior is most likely to belong to what type of ethnic community?

    A. Asian-American
    B. Latino
    C. Native American
    D. African-American

5. A community's infant mortality is best described as deaths occurring in the first _____ months of life for every 1,000 live births.

    A. 2   B. 6   C. 12   D. 18

6. Vital statistics can best be described as

    A. the percentage of dead or dying persons to living persons in a community
    B. the science of matter in equilibrium
    C. the science of health and its preservation
    D. a branch of biometry which deals with the data and laws of human mortality, morbidity, and demography

7. In large urban areas, which of the following represents the most effective means of controlling atmospheric dust?

    A. Controlling humidity
    B. Street cleaning
    C. Limiting combustion
    D. Limiting growth of ragweed and other heavy pollen producers

8. Which of the following variables is most significant in determining the total energy needs of a client?

   A. Age
   B. Physical activity
   C. Gender
   D. Nutritional status

9. A nurse learns that a family's plumbing system is without *traps.* This will generally mean that the family

   A. may be exposed to sewer air and foul gases
   B. will not have insoluble waste matter filtered from their liquid waste
   C. may be risking an exposure to rats or other rodents that might enter the house through the plumbing system
   D. may experience backflows of sewage or wastewater

10. Which of the following is not a physiological response involved in Selye's general adaptation syndrome (GAS) to stressors?

    A. *Increased* potassium excretion
    B. *Decreased* mental acuity
    C. *Increased* blood flow to skeletal muscles
    D. *Decreased* urinary output

11. A client's diet is found to be lacking in iron. Eating from which of the following food combinations will most likely correct this deficiency?

    A. Beef liver and turnip greens
    B. Egg whites and molasses
    C. Oysters and milk
    D. Apricots and whole wheat

12. Which of the following is not considered to be a *lifestyle* disease?

    A. Cancer
    B. Cardiovascular disease
    C. Malaria
    D. Adult-onset diabetes

13. In teaching a diabetic client the proper method of self-administration of an injection, a nurse decides to first concentrate on encouraging the client to accept the need for the injections and overcoming his fear of them.
    In this case, the nurse can be said to be targeting the client's _____ learning domain.

    A. attentional
    B. affective
    C. cognitive
    D. psychomotor

14. _____ Americans appear to experience increased susceptibility to Crohn's disease.

    A. East Indian
    B. Mexican
    C. European
    D. Jewish

15. When teaching a mother about her newborn child, a nurse should explain that each of the following factors may predispose an infant to functional vomiting EXCEPT

    A. overdilution of formula
    B. lack of sufficient burping
    C. feeding with the child positioned vertically upright
    D. feeding too rapidly

16. Which of the following best describes the primary goal of a long-term rehabilitation program?

    A. Restoring the ability to exercise
    B. Training the client to perform the activities of daily life
    C. Correcting deformities that have developed
    D. Prevention of secondary complications

17. When applied to nursing, the concept of holism implies that when a nurse assesses one part of a client's health, the nurse must

    A. compare it to a standard established for clients with similar physical and physiological characteristics
    B. compare it to a standard established for clients with like demographic characteristics
    C. consider how that part's condition may affect the community in which the client lives
    D. consider how that part relates to all others associated with the client's health

18. It is generally thought best for adolescent girls who become pregnant to

    A. stay in a foster home until delivery of the child
    B. give the child up for adoption
    C. enter a maternity home for the last nine weeks before delivery
    D. stay at home throughout the pregnancy

19. What is the term for the philosophy of teaching a client what to expect before he begins to be troubled or make mistakes?

    A. Anticipatory guidance   B. Wellness training
    C. Health education   D. Aversion therapy

20. Which of the following is an early sign of vitamin C deficiency?

    A. Eczema   B. Bleeding gums
    C. Dizziness   D. Double vision

21. The basic idea behind the open systems model of nursing care is to use communication in order to

    A. involve the client's family in the care plan
    B. help the client reestablish a positive adaptation to the environment
    C. prevent illness
    D. cure illness

22. Which of the following statements about food poisoning is generally considered to be FALSE?

    A. Most outbreaks are caused by ptomaines.
    B. Certain cases may involve bacterial toxins.
    C. Botulism is among the types of food poisoning that affect the nervous system.
    D. Most types of food poisoning involve the symptom of gastrointestinal distress.

23. Which of the following scenarios would be least likely to create an imbalance in the variables involved in the host/agent/environment model of health?
A(n)

    A. individual is given a salary increase
    B. individual fatigued by insomnia
    C. sudden change in jobs
    D. rainy spell

24. The community in which a nurse practices experiences a relatively high incidence of goiter. The nurse should advise members of this community to include _____ in their meals.

    A. 7-grain bread   B. citrus
    C. egg yolks   D. seafood

25. In the United States, the most prominent system of organized care is

    A. health care   B. immunization
    C. illness care   D. welfare

KEY (CORRECT ANSWERS)

1. C		11. D	
2. C		12. C	
3. B		13. B	
4. B		14. D	
5. C		15. C	
6. D		16. B	
7. C		17. D	
8. B		18. D	
9. A		19. A	
10. B		20. B	

21. B
22. A
23. A
24. D
25. C

TEST 3

DIRECTIONS: Each question or incomplete statement is followed by several suggested answers or completions. Select the one that BEST answers the question or completes the statement. *PRINT THE LETTER OF THE CORRECT ANSWER IN THE SPACE AT THE RIGHT.*

1. A small amount of atmospheric particulate may be beneficial over both urban and rural areas because it   1.____

   A. screens out microorganisms
   B. filters some harmful ultraviolet rays
   C. encourages precipitation
   D. provides contrast for long-distance viewing

2. Of the following methods for fighting communicable diseases in a community, which is most effective?   2.____

   A. Enforcing laws requiring the reporting of communicable diseases
   B. Imposing a quarantine period on all incoming citizens
   C. Conducting a vigorous vaccination and immunization program
   D. Promoting and teaching an extensive dietary and exercise program

3. If several children from the same family are to be examined on the same day, the _____ child should always be examined first.   3.____

   A. oldest
   B. youngest
   C. least anxious
   D. most anxious

4. Which of the following is/are most likely to be considered acts of secondary prevention?   4.____

   A. Immunization
   B. Preventing complications
   C. Enhancing rehabilitation
   D. Screening techniques

5. The nurse should inform the pregnant woman who is diabetic that children born to diabetic mothers are susceptible to   5.____

   A. hip dysplasia
   B. hyaline membrane disease
   C. Rh disease
   D. imperforate anus

6. A 40-year-old male client is admitted to the emergency room after suffering a broken leg in an automobile accident. The client is uninsured and has recently begun a job as a line worker in a factory. He is married with four children, and is unsure of his new employer's policy concerning injuries that are not related to his new job. The nurse in charge of the client's care begins the care plan by determining which medical and psychological factors may create obstacles to the client's caring for himself. The nurse is applying the _____ model of nursing.   6.____

   A. conservation principles
   B. adaptation
   C. systems
   D. environmental

7. A diet that overemphasizes milk is most likely to lead to a(n) _____ deficiency in the diet of a child.   7.____

   A. potassium
   B. calcium
   C. vitamin D
   D. iron

33

8. European Americans tend to experience a higher incidence of _____ than other ethnic/ racial groups in the United States.

   A. breast cancer
   B. hypertension
   C. lactose intolerance
   D. glaucoma

   8.____

9. On inspecting a family's house for health risks, a community nurse notices that the kitchen sink faucet is curved sharply, dipping down into the basin below the rim of the sink. The nurse should advise the family to correct this situation in order to eliminate the possibility of

   A. the unclean surface of the faucet contacting the water in the sink
   B. interfering with the sink's proper drainage
   C. the suctioning of wastewater back into the supply of drinkable water
   D. overflow and subsequent puddling

   9.____

10. The leading cause of morbidity and mortality in infants is

    A. accidents
    B. chemically induced deformities or disabilities
    C. congenital heart defects
    D. infections

    10.____

11. When applying Maslow's hierarchy to nursing care, it is important to remember that the

    A. caregiver must always take modifying factors into account
    B. focus of care should always be on the client's current needs, rather than strict adherence to the hierarchy
    C. hierarchy is not typically relevant to tertiary care
    D. client's self-esteem needs must never be given priority over physiological needs

    11.____

12. In general, mothers aged _____ have the lowest risk for maternal mortality.

    A. 12-20   B. 20-30   C. 30-40   D. 40-50

    12.____

13. If a client is encouraged to perform monthly self-examinations of her breasts, the nurse should teach her to position herself

    A. lying on the side opposite the breast being examined, with the hand of the arm on the examined side at the waist
    B. with the shoulder of the examined side flat on the bed, with the arm above the head
    C. with the shoulder of the examined side propped on a small pillow and the arm raised to about 70 degrees
    D. with the shoulder of the examined side propped on a small pillow and the opposite arm crossing over the abdomen

    13.____

14. A community's water supply is routinely examined for the presence of coliform bacteria, for the primary reason that this test is used to determine

    A. the presence of typhoid bacteria
    B. general drinkability
    C. the likelihood of dysentery-causing organisms
    D. the presence of fecal pollution

    14.____

15. The primary sociological factor involved in community and family health is 15.____

    A. spiritual beliefs   B. family unit size
    C. poverty   D. ethnicity

16. A deficiency in vitamin D will be most apparent in its effects on a client's _____ system. 16.____

    A. skeletal   B. circulatory
    C. muscular   D. integumentary

17. In terms of nursing care, a focus on the population would be most legitimate for 17.____

    A. program planning   B. individual care
    C. preventing illness   D. family intervention

18. At what time in a person's life is the potential for growth typically greatest? 18.____

    A. Late adolescence   B. Early adolescence
    C. Late childhood   D. Early childhood

19. A nurse should instruct a client that when washing dishes, glasses in which milk has been served should be 19.____

    A. scrubbed with an abrasive solution
    B. rinsed first with cold water
    C. washed in a mild bleach solution
    D. rinsed first with boiling water

20. Just prior to having her temperature taken for an initial nursing assessment, a client has been smoking. How many minutes should the nurse wait before taking an oral temperature? 20.____

    A. 10   B. 15   C. 20   D. 30

21. Which of the following strategies for preventing maternal deprivation in a community would typically be most effective? 21.____

    A. Improving the school environment
    B. Practicing early detection and special attention to high-risk children
    C. Expanding institutional and foster care programs
    D. Expanding the adoption network

22. Halpert Dunn's conception of *high-level wellness* could best be described as 22.____

    A. the ability to care for one's self
    B. an ongoing process, directed toward higher potential
    C. a concrete goal aimed at factors particular to the client's current situation
    D. the absence of illness

23. Communities which do not have access to a public water system are most likely to experience a deficiency in 23.____

    A. calcium   B. fluoride
    C. hydrogen ions   D. chloride

24. Which of the following is LEAST likely to be a factor in determining a family unit's vulnerability to health problems?

    A. Family developmental level
    B. Number of people in the nuclear family unit
    C. Age of family members
    D. Life-style practices

25. Each of the following factors is known to predispose a pregnant woman to toxemia EXCEPT

    A. diabetes with renal involvement
    B. multiple gestations
    C. African-American descent
    D. positive Rh factor

KEY (CORRECT ANSWERS)

1.	C	11.	B
2.	A	12.	B
3.	C	13.	C
4.	D	14.	D
5.	B	15.	C
6.	C	16.	A
7.	D	17.	A
8.	A	18.	B
9.	C	19.	B
10.	C	20.	B

21.	B
22.	B
23.	B
24.	B
25.	D

TEST 4

DIRECTIONS: Each question or incomplete statement is followed by several suggested answers or completions. Select the one that BEST answers the question or completes the statement. *PRINT THE LETTER OF THE CORRECT ANSWER IN THE SPACE AT THE RIGHT.*

1. By what means is chemically pure water most usually produced? 1.____

   A. Filtration B. Distillation
   C. Flocculation D. Boiling

2. Which of the following factors is LEAST likely to contribute to infant mortality? 2.____

   A. Time period between births
   B. Number of siblings
   C. Mother's age
   D. Low birth weight

3. According to Maslow's hierarchy of needs, which of the following types of needs are typically considered most basic to a client's health? 3.____

   A. Physiological B. Self-esteem
   C. Love and belonging D. Safety and security

4. Smoky or smoggy air in a community is most likely to create health problems associated with 4.____

   A. interfering with visibility, contributing to accidents
   B. blocking sunlight from reaching the earth
   C. contamination of textiles and household linens
   D. destroying nearby vegetation

5. When planning a teaching program for diabetic clients, which of the following is likely to be most effective? 5.____

   A. Analyzing each diabetic's history
   B. Planning to teach clients just prior to discharge
   C. Emphasizing dietary concerns above all else
   D. Holding each teaching program to a single standard

6. A low-income family produces and cans much of its own food. Members of this family should be reminded that the most unstable vitamin to storage is vitamin 6.____

   A. A B. B C. C D. E

7. In terms of the community, the most important reason for prevention and control of the common cold and flu is 7.____

   A. the lack of specific treatment for these illnesses
   B. the possibility of serious complications
   C. the economic loss caused by work absence
   D. a high mortality rate associated with epidemics

8. A client complains that she is unable to drink milk without developing diarrhea. The nurse should be aware that lactose intolerance is experienced at an unusually high rate among

   A. Eastern European Americans
   B. Native Americans
   C. East Indians
   D. African Americans

9. Which of the following ethnic/racial groups appears to experience increased susceptibility to diabetes mellitus?

   A. Mexican Americans
   B. Haitian/Caribbean Americans
   C. Arctic natives
   D. Chinese Americans

10. During the first two months of life, an infant's muscle tone should be expected to be primarily

    A. flexor   B. extensor   C. adductor   D. abductor

11. In caring for a client, a nurse following Pender's model of health promotion would direct his efforts toward

    A. determining the root causes of illness
    B. developing individual resources that enhance well-being
    C. assessing the strength of the client's family
    D. limiting risk factors that impede wellness

12. Each of the following groups of women would be classified as high-risk for possible pregnancy outcomes EXCEPT women

    A. with one living child, experiencing their second pregnancy
    B. of low socioeconomic status
    C. weighing less than 110 pounds
    D. experiencing their first pregnancy

13. Which of the following methods of assessing a client's mental status is typically most effective?

    A. Using responses to a list of questions prepared in advance
    B. Asking the client to describe his mental status
    C. Observing reactions to provocative questions
    D. Observing the client during the interview and examination

14. A family relies heavily on canned goods for their daily meals. Which of the following should be considered to be most indicative of spoiled contents in cans?

    A. Cans that are dented
    B. Convex ends to the cans
    C. Rusted cans
    D. Concave ends to the cans

15. An important limitation in applying Erickson's psycho-social development theory to nursing care is that it

    A. places a heavy emphasis on sexual behaviors
    B. doesn't relate specific tasks to appropriate ages
    C. doesn't address cognitive or moral development
    D. ignores biological factors

16. Which of the following constitutes the leading cause of death in the United States?

    A. Accidents in the home
    B. Automobile accidents
    C. Cancer
    D. Occupational accidents

17. Each of the following conditions should lead a nurse to suspect prediabetes in a female client EXCEPT

    A. abnormal glucose tolerance tests
    B. a history of hypertension
    C. hydramnios
    D. a history of stillborns

18. Which of the following types of ethnic communities in the United States is most likely to include a large number of families with a female head of household?

    A. Arab-American
    B. Chinese-American
    C. African-American
    D. Latino

19. Which of the following would be the equivalent of one slice of bread on the diabetic exchange lists?

    A. One bowl of cereal
    B. One baked potato
    C. 1/3 cup corn
    D. 1/2 glass milk

20. An *agent*, according to the host/agent/environment model of health, is

    A. a person carrying a communicable disease
    B. a factor external to the host that may or may not predispose a person to the development of a disease
    C. a person who may or may not be at risk for acquiring a disease
    D. any factor or stressor that can lead to illness or disease by means of its presence or absence

21. Common table salt, in the right concentrations, acts as a food preservative by

    A. dehydrating the cells of the food being preserved, giving microorganisms no reason to remain
    B. dehydrating the cells of microorganisms, causing their death
    C. dissolving in water to produce a weak solution of bactericidal hydrochloric acid
    D. reacting chemically with proteins in the food and making them more resistant to microorganisms

22. Which of the following is a nursing diagnosis involving health perception/management according to Gordon's functional health patterns?

    A. Altered growth and development in health
    B. High risk altered body temperature
    C. Activity intolerance
    D. Spiritual distress

23. According to Kruger (1991), the areas of nurse responsibility in client education include each of the following EXCEPT

    A. documentation of client activities
    B. preparation of clients receiving care
    C. use of standardized learning objectives
    D. preparation of clients being discharged from a health care facility

24. A nurse's personal philosophy holds birth control to be immoral. For professional practice, the nurse should

    A. explain her personal beliefs before discussing birth control with a client
    B. respect the beliefs of others who do not share her beliefs
    C. ensure that the client understands that decisions concerning birth control must necessarily involve some moral considerations
    D. ask another nurse to provide birth control counseling if a situation presents itself

25. Direct sunlight is considered to be germicidal because of its

    A. ultraviolet rays
    B. yellow visible-spectrum light
    C. heat-carrying properties
    D. infrared rays

KEY (CORRECT ANSWERS)

1. B		11. B	
2. B		12. A	
3. A		13. D	
4. B		14. B	
5. A		15. C	
6. C		16. A	
7. C		17. B	
8. D		18. C	
9. A		19. C	
10. A		20. D	

21. B
22. A
23. C
24. B
25. A

EXAMINATION SECTION
TEST 1

DIRECTIONS: Each question or incomplete statement is followed by several suggested answers or completions. Select the one that BEST answers the question or completes the statement. *PRINT THE LETTER OF THE CORRECT ANSWER IN THE SPACE AT THE RIGHT.*

1. The most important natural barrier that helps people to prevent the entry of pathogens is   1.____

    A. mucus
    B. T cells
    C. cilia
    D. the skin

2. A patient has right-sided weakness. When dressing the patient in a blouse, the nursing assistant should   2.____

    A. put it on the right side first
    B. put it on the left side first
    C. pull it over the head and put both arms through at once
    D. put the right arm in a sling

3. Of the following, the activity most likely to be considered a secondary-prevention activity would be   3.____

    A. immunization
    B. preventing complications
    C. enhancing rehabilitation
    D. screening

4. Which of the following activities would generally burn the most kilo-calories per hour?   4.____

    A. Cross-country skiing
    B. Bicycling
    C. Canoeing
    D. Swimming

5. Which of the following is considered to be a kind of restraint?   5.____

    A. Gait belt
    B. Abductor wedge
    C. Posey vest
    D. Cannula

6. A patient has redness and clear drainage from her right eye. The medical abbreviation for right eye is   6.____

    A. O.D.
    B. R.E.
    C. O.S.
    D. E.R.

7. A nursing assistant has stored a disinfected batch of equipment in the supply closet. The disinfection would be invalidated by

   A. removing the equipment for use in another unit
   B. damage or water penetration of the packaging
   C. the movement of the equipment to another location in supply
   D. removing prepackaged items with ungloved hands

8. Direct nursing care is an element of the_____ stage of the nursing process.

   A. implementation
   B. assessment
   C. diagnosis
   D. evaluation

9. Vital signs include
   I. weight
   II. body temperature
   III. pulse rate
   IV. respiratory rate

   A. I and II
   B. I, II and III
   C. II, III and IV
   D. I, II, III and IV

10. A patient"s diet is found to be thiamin-deficient. Which of the following dietary elements would serve as the best remedy?

    A. Fruit
    B. Bread or cereal
    C. Beans
    D. Dairy products

11. Which of the following is NOT typically a physiological manifestation of stress?

    A. Pale skin
    B. Decreased urinary output
    C. Decreased blood sugar
    D. Dry mouth

12. A nursing assistant is preparing a patient for ambulation. Which of the following precautions is appropriate?

    A. Dressing the patient in clothing of his or her choosing
    B. Ensuring that the patient is not dizzy or disoriented
    C. Placing a towel over any spills on the floor
    D. Checking to see if the patient can stand alone before offering assistance

13. In the nursing process, _____ are stated goals for health care activities that can be used to plan and evaluate care.   13._____

    A. quality assurances
    B. audits
    C. standards of care
    D. criteria

14. A patient diagnosed with chronic pain may exhibit the defining characteristic of   14._____

    A. communication of pain descriptors
    B. altered muscle tone
    C. physical and social withdrawal
    D. guarded, protective behavior

15. The purpose of a turning sheet is to   15._____

    A. substitute for another person if nobody is available to move a helpless or heavy patient
    B. reduce friction when moving helpless or heavy patients
    C. serve as a light restraint while the patient's bed is being changed
    D. relieve pressure while supporting the patient's body

16. Of following patient positions, which typically promotes maximal chest expansion?   16._____

    A. Orthopneic
    B. Sims'
    C. Trendelenburg
    D. High Fowler's

17. Range of motion exercises can help   17._____
    I. increase aerobic capacity
    II. prevent contractures
    III. increase muscular strength
    IV. improve circulation

    A. I and II
    B. I and IV
    C. II, III and IV
    D. I, II, III and IV

18. _____ infections are associated with the delivery of health care services in a health care facility.   18._____

    A. Vector
    B. Nosocomial
    C. Exogenous
    D. Complementary

19. Each of the following is an appropriate action to take in caring for a patient with cancer, EXCEPT

    A. keeping the patient's skin clean, dry and pressure-free
    B. using surgical asepsis for infection control
    C. remaining positive and listening to the patient's concerns
    D. providing emotional support after hair loss

19.____

20. The FIRST stage of the nursing process is

    A. planning
    B. evaluation
    C. diagnosis
    D. assessment

20.____

21. Each of the following is typically involved in the nutritional assessment of a patient, EXCEPT

    A. measuring mid-upper arm circumference
    B. comparing weight to body build
    C. girth measurements
    D. a dietary history

21.____

22. Of the stages involved in death outlined by Elizabeth Kubler Ross, the last is usually

    A. acceptance
    B. depression
    C. denial
    D. anger

22.____

23. Of the following foods,_____ would most effectively boost the vitamin B content of a patient's diet.

    A. fruits
    B. dairy products
    C. simple sugars
    D. poultry

23.____

24. When changing unsterile dressing, the nursing assistant should wash hands
    I. before the procedure
    II. after removing the soiled dressing
    III. after the completion of the procedure

    A. I only
    B. II only
    C. II and III
    D. I, II and III

24.____

25. Which of the following would be a care consideration for maintaining the comfort of an elderly patient?

    A. Ensuing privacy
    B. Maintaining the patient's body temperature at a level that is agreeable
    C. Teaching about facility policies and procedures
    D. Allowing familiar caregivers access to the patient

KEY (CORRECT ANSWERS)

1.	D	11.	C
2.	A	12.	B
3.	D	13.	C
4.	A	14.	C
5.	C	15.	B
6.	A	16.	A
7.	B	17.	C
8.	A	18.	B
9.	C	19.	B
10.	B	20.	D

21. C
22. A
23. D
24. D
25. B

TEST 2

DIRECTIONS: Each question or incomplete statement is followed by several suggested answers or completions. Select the one that BEST answers the question or completes the statement. *PRINT THE LETTER OF THE CORRECT ANSWER IN THE SPACE AT THE RIGHT.*

1. Which of the following positions is used specifically to relax tension of the patient's abdominal muscles?

    A. Knee-chest
    B. Trendelenburg
    C. Sim's
    D. Fowler's

    1.____

2. Approximately_____ percent of an average American's energy intake is derived from carbohydrates.

    A. 15
    B. 45
    C. 65
    D. 80

    2.____

3. When caring for a patient with a Foley catheter, it is important to

    A. remove the catheter for frequent inspection
    B. attach the drainage bag to the side rail of the bed
    C. empty the drainage bag at the beginning of every shift
    D. keep the drainage bag below the bladder

    3.____

4. The Joint Commission on Accreditation of Healthcare Organizations (JCAHO) requires that, in order to reduce the risk of falls, health care facilities such as hospitals should

    A. avoid prescribing medications that may contribute to falls
    B. educate patients about the dangers inherent in many medications
    C. establish a fall-reduction program and evaluate its effectiveness
    D. restrain patients who are at a high risk for falling

    4.____

5. Macronutrients include each of the following, EXCEPT

    A. carbohydrates
    B. fats
    C. proteins
    D. minerals

    5.____

6. A person's body temperature is
    I. lowest in the morning
    II. higher during infection in older patients than in younger patients
    III. highest in the afternoon or evening
    IV. most appropriately measured with a glass thermometer

    A. I only
    B. I and III
    C. II, III and IV
    D. I, II, III and IV

7. A patient who is at risk for pressure sores should have a systematic skin inspection at least

    A. every 4 hours
    B. twice daily
    C. daily
    D. every 2 days

8. A patient has experienced some hearing loss. In order to communicate clearly with the patient, a nurse should

    A. speak while looking directly at the patient
    B. use simple hand gestures
    C. speaking loudly and slowly
    D. speak in a higher pitch than normal

9. A nursing assistant is teaching a patient how to perform range-of-motion exercises independently. He should instruct the patient to do each of the following, EXCEPT

    A. perform each exercise to the point of slight resistance
    B. perform each exercise three times
    C. vary the sequence of the exercises from day to day
    D. perform each series of exercises twice daily

10. Which of the following is a method of cleaning equipment with chemicals or boiling water?

    A. Sterilization
    B. Disinfection
    C. Decontamination
    D. Antisepsis

11. The best explanation for the relatively higher incidence of obesity in low-income communities is related to

    A. the food preferences of cultural or ethnic groups who predominate these populations
    B. a tendency to purchase greater amounts of pre-processed foods
    C. a greater reliance on daily products
    D. a reliance on cheaper cuts of meat

12. The following steps to turning a patient from his back to his side in bed, in their proper order, are
    I. With your back straight and knees bent, pull the person toward you.
    II. Put both of your arms under the patient's waist and hips. Pull the hips toward you so the buttocks stick out a little.
    III. Put one arm under the patient's hips and the other under his up per back
    IV. Gently push to lift the hip and shoulder off the bed until the patient is resting on the hip and shoulder farthest from you.

    A. I, II, III, IV
    B. II, IV, III, I
    C. III, I, IV, II
    D. III, IV, I, II

13. A nurse is assessing a patient's ability to achieve wellness, applying the model of health promotion developed by Nola Pender. Which of the following would be considered a modifying factor involved in the patient's ability to participate in health-promoting behavior?

    A. The influence of the patient's family
    B. The patient's perceived level of control over his or her health
    C. The barriers that the patient perceives to health-promoting behavior
    D. The overall importance of health to the patient

14. The development of goals and objectives is an aspect of the _____ stage of the nursing process.

    A. assessment
    B. planning
    C. implementation
    D. evaluation

15. A patient is unresponsive. How many initial breaths should be administered before checking the pulse?

    A. 2
    B. 3
    C. 4
    D. 6

16. A patient is dying. The last sensory input she will lose will be her

    A. taste
    B. smell
    C. sight
    D. hearing

17. _____ precautions require the use of personal protective equipment within 3 feet of the patient

    A. Enteric
    B. Droplet
    C. Airborne
    D. Contact

18. Which of the following is the term for a sheet that is placed crosswise over the bottom sheet in the middle of a bed?

    A. Turning sheet
    B. Top sheet
    C. Drawsheet
    D. Transfer sheet

19. When transferring a patient, most of the patient's weight should be supported by the nursing assistant's

    A. shoulders
    B. upper arms
    C. legs
    D. back

20. A vaccination is an example of _____ health problem prevention.

    A. primary
    B. secondary
    C. tertiary
    D. prophylactic

21. A patient and a nurse are discussing the possibility of beginning a routine of moderate physical activity. The patient, who has been inactive for a long time, is concerned about the possibility of adverse effects. The most common adverse effect of physical activity is

    A. dizziness and anxiety
    B. cardiac arrest
    C. chronic fatigue
    D. musculoskeletal injury

22. If the diet of a child relies excessively on milk, the child is most at risk for a(n) _____ deficiency.

    A. calcium
    B. vitamin A
    C. vitamin D
    D. iron

23. When cleaning and disinfecting objects, nursing professionals should be led by each of the following guidelines, EXCEPT

    A. for the initial rinse, use hot water
    B. wash with hot water and soap
    C. for the final rinse, use warm water
    D. use an abrasive to clean equipment with grooves and corners

24. When treating a patient with pressure sores, the head of the bed should be elevated to a maximum angle of _____ degrees.

    A. 5
    B. 15
    C. 30
    D. 45

25. If a patient is isolated under enteric precautions, the purpose is usually to prevent

    A. infections transmitted by direct or indirect contact with infected blood or serae
    B. infections transmitted through direct or indirect contact with feces
    C. highly transmissible infections not requiring strict isolation but spread by close or direct contact
    D. stomach upset

KEY (CORRECT ANSWERS)

1. D		11. B	
2. B		12. C	
3. D		13. A	
4. C		14. B	
5. D		15. A	
6. B		16. D	
7. C		17. B	
8. A		18. C	
9. C		19. C	
10. B		20. A	

21. D
22. D
23. A
24. C
25. B

TEST 3

DIRECTIONS: Each question or incomplete statement is followed by several suggested answers or completions. Select the one that BEST answers the question or completes the statement. *PRINT THE LETTER OF THE CORRECT ANSWER IN THE SPACE AT THE RIGHT.*

1. The phrase "fifth vital sign" usually refers to

    A. blood glucose
    B. emotional distress
    C. functional status
    D. pain

2. Falls among elderly patients most commonly occur during activities that

    A. require physical dexterity
    B. are part of the person's daily routine
    C. involve high aerobic demands
    D. are risky and beyond the person's capabilities

3. A physician asks the nursing assistant to place a patient in the Sims' position. The patient should be

    A. in a semi-upright sitting position with the knees bent
    B. flat on the back with the head lower than the pelvis
    C. on her left side, left leg extended and right leg flexed
    D. in a kneeling position, supported by the knees and the shoulders, with the chest sagging down

4. Protective gloves should be used

    A. whenever one is within three feet of a patient
    B. only when directly handling specimens
    C. when there is actual, observable contact with blood or body fluids
    D. any time one is likely to touch a patient

5. The most common infecting organism associated with nosocomial infections is

    A. Enterococcus
    B. Staphylococcus aureus
    C. Lactobacillus
    D. E. coli

6. Each of the following is an important priority of data collection during the assessment stage of the nursing process, EXCEPT

    A. communicating with the patient, rather than consulting secondary sources
    B. including information about both strengths and needs
    C. arranging results in a way that is easily retrievable by future researchers
    D. including the patient's responses to current alterations

7. Signs of cerebrovascular problems include
   I. numbness
   II. blurred vision
   III. dizziness
   IV. shortness of breath

   A. I and II
   B. I, II, and III
   C. II and IV
   D. I, II, III and IV

8. The primary, secondary and tertiary levels of preventive action are elements of the_____ phase of the nursing process.

   A. assessment
   B. planning
   C. intervention
   D. evaluation

9. A patient is upset and crying about the recent death of his spouse. The most appropriate response to this would be to

   A. point out all the good things the patient can appreciate in his life
   B. leave the patient alone in his grief
   C. suggest some activities that might help the patient take his mind off things
   D. sit with the patient and allow him to talk about his feelings if he wishes

10. The performance of the Heinilich maneuver requires placement of the thumb

    A. just below the navel
    B. just above the navel
    C. right below the lower end of the sternum
    D. in the center of the sternum

11. A patient's dietary orders require that he receive a certain number of milliliters of juice. The container is a four ounce container. In order to determine the number of milliliters in the container, the nursing assistant should

    A. divide 30 by 4
    B. divide 60 by 4
    C. multiply 4 by 30
    D. multiply 4 by 60

12. A nursing assistant is putting a patient to bed for the night. Which of the following would NOT be a safety measure that should be taken?

    A. Using side rails
    B. Providing long intravenous tubing
    C. Using night-lights
    D. Placing the bed in a high position

13. At the primary level, health problem prevention is concerned with

    A. preventing the occurrence of health problems.
    B. discovering and treating existing health problems.
    C. easing the pain of existing, terminal health problems.
    D. reducing the severity of existing health problems.

14. "Nutrition" is most accurately defined as

    A. the kinds of food that a person habitually eats
    B. the sum of all the interactions between a person and the food he or she consumes
    C. the assimilation of food, through the stomach and bowels, into the body's organ systems
    D. the biochemical and physiologic processes by which the body grows and maintains itself

15. A nurse attempts to meet patient needs by applying Maslow's hierarchy to nursing care. In doing this, it is important for the health care professional to remember that the

    A. professional must always take modifying factors into account
    B. care should always focus on the patient's current needs, rather than strict adherence to the theoretical hierarchy
    C. hierarchy is not typically relevant to tertiary care
    D. patient's self-esteem needs must never be given priority over physiological needs

16. OSHA recommends that hypodermic needles should not be recapped if it can be avoided; however, if it is necessary, recapping should be performed using

    A. both hands
    B. at least one other person
    C. the one-handed "scoop" method
    D. puncture-proof gloves

17. Piaget's theory of cognitive development may be helpful to nurses in health promotion, in that it can help nurses to

    A. understand how children of various ages interpret health and health care
    B. identify the basic physical and psychosocial needs of children
    C. provide a basis for the assessment of a child's moral code
    D. provide a patient with tools to crisis-coping tools

18. To be sure that he is measuring a patient's weight accurately, a nursing assistant should weigh the patient

    A. at a different time each day
    B. after a meal
    C. after a nap
    D. at the same time every day

19. A patient and a nurse are discussing the patient's physical activity regimen. The patient wonders when would be the best time to perform stretching exercises. In order to increase flexibility, the best time to stretch is

    A. during moderate physical activity
    B. when checking the pulse
    C. during the post-exercise cool-down
    D. about an hour before exercising

20. The nursing assessment of a patient's nutritional status typically involves a dietary history of the patient's previous

    A. 24 hours
    B. 3 days
    C. week
    D. 2 weeks

21. A patient is deaf. The best way to communicate with her would be to

    A. use simple hand gestures
    B. speak loudly
    C. write out information
    D. speak slowly to allow for lip-reading

22. A nursing assistant is helping an immobilized patient to perform passive range-of-motion exercises. Which of the following would NOT be a guideline for this procedure?

    A. If contracture is present, the exercises should be stopped immediately.
    B. Body parts should be moved slowly. Move the body parts slowly
    C. Only the limb being exercised should be exposed.
    D. If rigidity occurs, pressure should be applied against the rigidity and the exercise slowly continued.

23. A nursing assistant has become annoyed with a patient's extreme depression and negativity, and is having a hard time viewing him objectively. In this situation, the most appropriate action would be to

    A. gently suggest that there are other patients in the same unit whose situations are more difficult
    B. excuse oneself and calm down outside the room, if doing so poses no risk to the patient
    C. confront the patient about the unhelpfulness of his attitude
    D. remind the patient that emotions and attitude can have a direct effect on one's health

24. The nursing history of an assessment that is concerned with infection risk will typically involve questioning the patient about each of the following, EXCEPT

    A. physical activity
    B. urinary frequency or difficulty
    C. appetite
    D. nausea

25. The CDC, to encourage greater participation in physical activity, recommends that people engage in a minimum of

    A. 60 minutes of high-intensity physical activity at least 3 days a week
    B. 60 minutes of moderate-intensity physical activity on most days of the week
    C. 30 minutes of moderate-intensity physical activity on most days of the week
    D. 30 minutes of light-intensity physical activity every day

25.____

KEY (CORRECT ANSWERS)

1.	D	11.	C
2.	B	12.	D
3.	C	13.	A
4.	C	14.	B
5.	D	15.	B
6.	C	16.	C
7.	B	17.	A
8.	B	18.	D
9.	D	19.	C
10.	B	20.	A

21. C
22. A
23. B
24. A
25. C

EXAMINATION SECTION
TEST 1

DIRECTIONS: Each question or incomplete statement is followed by several suggested answers or completions. Select the one that BEST answers the question or completes the statement. *PRINT THE LETTER OF THE CORRECT ANSWER IN THE SPACE AT THE RIGHT.*

1. The general principles a nurse should follow to aid in the prevention of destructive outbursts in elderly people include all of the following EXCEPT   1._____

    A. discussing with the patient factors that stimulate hostility or aggression and giving argument to resolve conflicts
    B. never threatening, scolding, punishing, or shaming the person
    C. redirecting troublesome behavior into constructive channels
    D. quietly giving short, simple, direct responses to prevent additional confusion

2. Depression may alter patterns and styles of daily living. Depression generally does NOT cause   2._____

    A. erratic sleeping patterns varying from insomnia to excessive sleep
    B. a decrease in somatic complaints
    C. withdrawal from friends, family, and environment
    D. talk of suicide or suicide attempts

3. Short-term memory has a small capacity and is useful for almost instantaneous recollection.   3._____
Factors that increase the risk of short-term memory loss include all of the following EXCEPT

    A. shortened sensory overload
    B. CNS or circulatory deficits
    C. poor nutritional status
    D. hearing losses and visual deficits

4. Early in short-term memory loss, older persons may engage in behavior to cover for memory losses.   4._____
Later manifestations of more severe memory loss in elderly persons include

    A. failure to recognize when clothing is soiled, forgetting to bathe, wearing clothing longer than has been normal for them
    B. forgetting to prepare food or to eat
    C. forgetting to take medications according to regimen
    D. all of the above

5. Some older people create difficulties in daily living, not only for themselves, but also for all those around them.   5._____
All of the following are guidelines that caregivers and family members can use in dealing with these negative individuals EXCEPT:

    A. Set realistic goals with the person and be constructive
    B. Do not get the person involved in doing an activity

C. Accept the deprecating, complaining behavior, but continue to recognize positive contributions and outcomes, even as the person negates them
D. Agree on an approach in which all staff members and family members will behave consistently in responding to specified behavior

6. Nursing management of loneliness should never take a shotgun approach. Any intervention needs to be based on a validated diagnosis of the presence of loneliness plus the individual's

   A. times of greatest discomfort or risk
   B. goals for human intimacy
   C. current coping behavior
   D. all of the above

7. Diagnostic criteria for alcohol abuse does NOT include

   A. alcohol needed when an extra amount of work, besides the normal daily activities, needs to be done
   B. inability to cut down or stop drinking
   C. amnestic periods for events occurring while intoxicated
   D. continuation of drinking despite a serious physical disorder that the individual knows is exacerbated by alcohol use

8. Alcoholism in the elderly contributes to skeletal defects by causing

   A. osteoporosis
   B. risk of fractures through trauma
   C. both of the above
   D. none of the above

9. There are several conditions occurring in the central nervous system that are closely associated with long-term alcohol abuse.
   These include all of the following EXCEPT

   A. cerebellar degeneration
   B. amyotropic lateral sclerosis
   C. central pontine myelinolysis
   D. pallegra

10. Regarding common drugs and their interactions with alcohol, the use of _____ increases the risk of hypotension.

    A. nitroglycerin
    B. monoamine oxidase
    C. both of the above
    D. none of the above

11. Cancer of the colon and rectum are found most often in the elderly.
    Changes in bowel habits and character of stool require the older person to be a good observer and historian, as well as one who can remember other coexisting factors, including

    A. amount of water and other fluids taken during the time period
    B. types of food eaten, for example, fatty foods, no protein, high proteins, or only carbohydrates
    C. changes in activities and exercise patterns
    D. all of the above

12. In cancer detection approaches in the elderly, _____ may be used to detect cancer of the breast.   12.____

    A. breast self-examination
    B. mammography
    C. both of the above
    D. none of the above

13. Some elderly persons temporarily or permanently lose their full ability to masticate, to move the food bolus to the posterior pharynx, or to swallow the bolus to a patent esophagus, stomach, and intestinal tract. Treatment factors that cause such dysfunctions include all of the following EXCEPT   13.____

    A. untreated malignancy or metastatic disease of the oropharynx, larynx, esophagus, or gastrointestinal tract
    B. implanted dentures
    C. trismus as a sequel to radiation, edema, or infection
    D. implanted iridium needles in the tongue or floor of the mouth

14. After exposure to an accumulation of 5,000 rads or a total body exposure of 1,000 rads, changes in composition and consistency of saliva occur and it becomes ropy and tenacious.
    These changes provide a positive environment for infection by   14.____

    A. candidiasis
    B. herpes simplex infection
    C. both of the above
    D. none of the above

15. Of the following people, those at LEAST risk for managing their daily nutrition in the face of pain and dysphagia are those who   15.____

    A. were previously malnourished as a consequence of alcoholism
    B. are taking excessive analgesics
    C. maintained poor oral hygiene prior to, during, and after delivery
    D. have a solitary lifestyle with few personal support symptoms

16. Nursing strategies useful in managing difficulties in eating include all of the following EXCEPT   16.____

    A. no analgesia prior to eating
    B. oral hygiene to remove debris, plaque, and tenacious secretions
    C. use of deglutition spoon or modified syringe for liquid diets
    D. considering the option of enteral feeding or hyperalimentation

17. A nurse evaluating the patients response to living each day with the inability to eat should collect data on the status of   17.____

    A. oropharyngeal tissues
    B. gingiva and the ability to wear dentures or partials
    C. eating and swallowing skills
    D. all of the above

18. In the over-70 age group, even uncomplicated and successful surgery for cancer results in prolonged low energy levels for almost a year. Certain factors can be predicted to produce periods of low energy.
    Of the following, the factor that does NOT produce low energy is

    A. presence of other decompensating chronic disease
    B. early stages of metastatic disease
    C. neoplastic diseases in which fatigue is an initial and ongoing feature
    D. insomnia or sleep interruptions

19. Emotional components that contribute to low energy in elderly persons with cancer include all of the following EXCEPT

    A. feeling abandoned by the family or health care providers
    B. pleasant interpersonal relationships
    C. tasks demanding prolonged activity or concentration
    D. social events

20. All of the following conditions or situations decrease the ability to tolerate pain EXCEPT

    A. presence of gastrointestinal symptoms, for example, nausea, vomiting, diarrhea, constipation, impactions
    B. constant weight loss or cachexia
    C. excessive sleep
    D. emotional upset, such as anxiety, depression, fear, and anger

21. The factors in cancer and its treatment that increase vulnerability to infection do NOT include

    A. breakdown of skin and mucosal barriers due to tumor mass or treatment modalities
    B. neutropenia and malnutrition
    C. increased phagocytic function of leukocytes
    D. impaired antibody production

22. The best treatment for infection in older persons with cancer is prevention. The nursing regimen for prevention includes involving the patient and family in all of the following EXCEPT

    A. learning safe handwashing and oral hygiene techniques and patterns
    B. starting with prophylactic antibiotics
    C. learning safe laundry techniques and the importance of changing particular items of clothing and bedding regularly
    D. learning how to clean humidifiers and respirators, oxygen tubing, or other treatment instruments used in daily care

23. The older person with cancer experiences multiple separations in daily living with the disease and its treatment. Persons well-equipped to handle the separations associated with cancer are those who

    A. feel helpless or hopeless
    B. live alone or have diminishing contact with family and friends, particularly age-mates or favorite people
    C. suffer severe pain or intractable nausea and vomiting
    D. none of the above

24. Drug treatment can increase the risk of congestive cardiac failure. Inadequate or over-zealous drug therapy can precipitate congestive heart failure.
Drugs with this potential to affect congestive cardiac and heart failure do NOT include

   A. beta-adrenergic blockers
   B. calcium channel blockers
   C. digoxin
   D. alcohol

25. The most severe complication associated with congestive heart failure is the development of other end-stage organ disease as a result of chronic perfusion reduction. The goals of treatment that nurses should keep in mind include all of the following EXCEPT

   A. increase cardiac preload
   B. reduce sodium and water retention
   C. improve contractility of heart
   D. reduce cardiac workload

KEY (CORRECT ANSWERS)

1. A	11. D
2. B	12. C
3. A	13. B
4. D	14. C
5. B	15. B
6. D	16. A
7. A	17. D
8. C	18. B
9. B	19. B
10. A	20. C

21. C
22. B
23. D
24. B
25. A

TEST 2

DIRECTIONS: Each question or incomplete statement is followed by several suggested answers or completions. Select the one that BEST answers the question or completes the statement. *PRINT THE LETTER OF THE CORRECT ANSWER IN THE SPACE AT THE RIGHT.*

1. In elderly patients with CHF, methods used to decrease cardiac workload include   1.____

    A. vasodilators to reduce peripheral vascular resistance
    B. weight reduction
    C. both of the above
    D. none of the above

2. Digitalis, a cardiac glycoside, is the standard treatment for increasing the force and   2.____
    velocity of each contraction. Factors that influence the individuals sensitivity to digitalis
    include

    A. fluid and electrolyte balance, particularly sodium and potassium
    B. concomitant drug therapies, for example, anti-arrhythmics, catecholamines
    C. altered thyroid or renal function
    D. all of the above

3. While all older persons are at risk for arterial occlusive disease, there are some factors   3.____
    that increase the risk, including all of the following EXCEPT

    A. being a female
    B. having diabetes mellitus
    C. being a smoker
    D. having a history of coronary artery disease or cerebrovascular disease

4. Complications associated with ischemic heart disease in the elderly do NOT include   4.____

    A. cardiac failure   B. thyrotoxicosis
    C. cardiac rupture   D. pulmonary embolism

5. The nursing goals of treatment for older persons with ischemic heart disease include   5.____

    A. increasing myocardial oxygen supply
    B. reducing myocardial oxygen demand
    C. both of the above
    D. none of the above

6. Arterial occlusive disease can range from inconvenience to a severely debilitating dis-   6.____
    ease with serious ischemia and infarction of tissues in the lower extremities.
    Treatment of arterial occlusive disease in the elderly includes all of the following
    EXCEPT

    A. slowing the progression of the disease
    B. increasing collateral circulation
    C. increasing the cardiac afterload
    D. maintaining skin integrity

7. Congestive cardiac failure and other cardiac pathology commonly results in shortness of breath and reduced strength and endurance.
   NOT included among the complications in daily living that may occur if it is not managed effectively is

   A. discouragement and depression leading to slow suicide by misuse of medications, sodium consumption, not eating, and self-neglect
   B. excessive sleepiness
   C. malnutrition secondary to anorexia and the inability to shop for or prepare food
   D. use of high sodium convenience food

7.____

8. Chronic congestive heart failure and its treatment affect appetite and digestion in several ways.
   Factors that increase the problems experienced with food and eating include all of the following EXCEPT

   A. hepatic engorgement and enlarged heart
   B. dyspnea and decreased energy for eating
   C. splenic infarction
   D. persistent electrolyte imbalance

8.____

9. Managing eating with the side effects of congestive heart failure can be predicted on the basis of the persons

   A. capacity and eternal resources for purchasing and preparing meals
   B. understanding and acceptance of diet as an important factor in health status and relative well-being
   C. desire to live
   D. all of the above

9.____

10. Failure to incorporate appropriate eating into daily living with congestive heart failure can produce a downward spiral in which not eating results in even lessened hunger and leads to all of the following EXCEPT

    A. growing weakness
    B. increasing hepatic and splenic failure
    C. infection
    D. growing cardiac and serum chemistry

10.____

11. Prognostic variables on managing daily living with leg pain and intermittent claudication include

    A. rate of progression of the disease and symptoms present
    B. older persons motivation to begin and continue a prescribed exercise program
    C. previous capacity to make adjustments in daily living
    D. all of the above

11.____

12. Inability to manage daily living effectively because of leg pain and intermittent claudication in an elderly patient with congestive heart failure will most likely NOT result in

    A. social isolation because of inability to get out
    B. ulceration, gangrene, failure to manage acute emergencies, and resultant amputation or death

12.____

C. an angry feeling towards the staff with homicidal ideation
D. malnutrition

13. The nursing regimen in a patient of congestive heart failure with leg pain and intermittent claudication includes planning with the older person or primary care-givers on specific management of daily living as it relates to all of the following EXCEPT

   A. keeping the leg acutely flexed at the hips to enhance circulation
   B. externally supporting leg tissues
   C. planning activities ahead to reduce unnecessary walking in daily chores
   D. planning for alternatives

14. EFFECTIVE management of daily living with symptomatic peripheral vascular disease can be evaluated in terms of the

   A. amount of walking that can be done prior to onset of pain
   B. maintenance of personal care and nutritional status
   C. status of personal feeling of well-being
   D. all of the above

15. In the elderly, leg ulcers heal very slowly, if at all. Deterrents to managing daily living effectively with leg ulcers and their treatment do NOT include

   A. extensive deep, bilateral or infected ulcers
   B. hyperesthesia in legs
   C. lack of assistance in wound care, chores, and transportation
   D. lack of money for supplies and medications

16. Nursing interventions in the management of daily living with leg ulcers include all of the following EXCEPT

   A. teaching dressing, soaking, and wound cleaning techniques as needed
   B. trying to adopt a sitting posture most of the time, keeping the legs down
   C. as debridement is very painful, analgesics can be taken before an office visit
   D. helping the person deal with the reality of the slowness of the healing of ulcers, despite the best of care

17. Certain older persons are at greater risk of managing daily living by not dealing with the signs and symptoms of transient ischemic attacks.
Of the following, the only people NOT at increased risk are those who

   A. are continuously talking about these minor complaints to the doctor
   B. attribute the signs and symptoms of transient ischemic attacks to aging
   C. have an unclear mental status
   D. are loners with few close associates to recognize changes in their physical and mental states

18. Good prognosis for the effective management of daily living in an elderly patient with transient ischemic attacks includes

   A. being totally preoccupied with the threat and risks of transient ischemic attacks
   B. having a backup support system
   C. having poor skills or an inadequate plan for reporting the symptoms experienced
   D. all of the above

19. Nursing interventions in an elderly patient with transient ischemic attacks addresses several areas of daily living. These interventions include all of the following activities EXCEPT

    A. encouraging or assisting the older person to find a physician or clinician in whom he has confidence
    B. locating the telephone at bedside
    C. encouraging the patient for sudden rapid changes of position and movement
    D. improving the safety of the environment in the home

20. Of the following individuals, those NOT at higher risk for not being able to manage daily living with altered speech and comprehension include those who

    A. live with people or in a community where there is little understanding of the dynamics of pathology
    B. were very non-verbal prior to their stroke
    C. go out in a community where their condition is not recognized or understood
    D. lack a consistent companion

21. A person who recovers from a major stroke faces a long rehabilitation period. Rationale for use of the evaluation flow sheet includes the desire to

    A. assess improvements of functions
    B. enhance self-esteem and body image
    C. recall how much progress has been made since the onset of disability
    D. all of the above

22. The cornerstone of treatment of diabetes mellitus is diet. The goal of diet treatment includes all of the following EXCEPT

    A. achievement and maintenance of ideal body weight
    B. taking concentrated carbohydrates
    C. avoidance of wide swings of blood pressure
    D. normal blood fats

23. Factors responsible for symptomatology of hypoglycemia in an elderly patient with diabetes mellitus include

    A. decreased glucose available to brain
    B. epinephrine release with a sympathetic nervous system response
    C. both of the above
    D. none of the above

24. Guidelines for the diabetic patient or for people responsible for the diabetic patient include:

    A. Inspecting feet daily for blisters, breaks, calluses, and bruises
    B. Washing with mild soap and then soaking in water for 15 minutes
    C. Avoiding stockings with holes or mended places
    D. All of the above

25. Helping an older person cope with diabetes is a complex situation. 25.____
A realistic look at the elderly person seems to justify adjustment of all of the following goals EXCEPT

    A. attainment and maintenance of ideal body weight
    B. presence of hypoglycemia
    C. absence of acidosis and ketonuria
    D. absence of atrophy or scarring of hypertrophy at injection sites

KEY (CORRECT ANSWERS)

1. C	11. D
2. D	12. C
3. A	13. A
4. B	14. D
5. C	15. B
6. C	16. B
7. B	17. A
8. C	18. B
9. D	19. C
10. B	20. B

21. D
22. B
23. C
24. D
25. B

EXAMINATION SECTION
TEST 1

DIRECTIONS: Each question or incomplete statement is followed by several suggested answers or completions. Select the one that BEST answers the question or completes the statement. *PRINT THE LETTER OF THE CORRECT ANSWER IN THE SPACE AT THE RIGHT.*

1. When developing a conceptual framework for nursing practice with the elderly, a nurse should resolve the question: What

    A. assumptions, beliefs, and values about nursing and the elderly influence my practice?
    B. is the range of expected health outcomes for older persons?
    C. is the nature of the professional nurse's relationship with other health care providers of the elderly?
    D. all of the above

    1.____

2. Much of gerontological nursing is application of nursing processes and methods, with special attention to the unique influences of the aging process on health and illness. Modifications in elements of nursing practice because patients are of advanced age include all of the following EXCEPT

    A. fast pace of nursing process
    B. attention to the effects of the aging process on disease presentation and responses to disease and treatment
    C. increased alertness for signs of an intensified stress state
    D. financial resources available to implement plan of care

    2.____

3. Dryness, wrinkling, laxity, uneven pigmentation, and a variety of proliferative lesions of the skin are due to normal aging, the genetic makeup of the individual, and environmental factors, such as sun exposure.
Lichenification is classified as nonpathologic skin lesions found in the elderly and characterized by

    A. well-circumscribed areas of cutaneous thickening and hardening
    B. results from repeated rubbing or scratching
    C. both of the above
    D. none of the above

    3.____

4. An estimated 40% of Americans 65-74 years of age suffer from a skin disease that is severe enough for them to seek treatment.
All of the following are common pathological skin lesions found in the elderly EXCEPT

    A. psoriasis   B. seborrheic keratoses
    C. herpes zoster   D. bullous pemphigoid

    4.____

5. The incidence of potentially blinding diseases increases dramatically after the age of 65. The one of the following that is NOT among the leading causes of blindness in elderly people is

    A. senile macular degeneration   B. senile angioma (cherry spot)
    C. senile cataract   D. acute angle closure glaucoma

    5.____

6. Breast cancer is the most common malignancy found in women and accounts for 2% of deaths in women over 75 years of age.
The BEST diagnostic procedure for breast screening in a woman over 50 years of age includes

   A. breast self-examination
   B. annual professional examination
   C. mammogram
   D. all of the above

7. The aging gut may be characterized by decreased secretions, absorption, and motility.
Of the following, the LEAST likely cause of severe abdominal pain is

   A. gallbladder disease, secondary to inflammation, obstruction, or cancer
   B. acute pancreatitis
   C. torsion of testis
   D. mesenteric thrombosis, infarction, or hemorrhage

8. The prevalence of colorectal cancer increases at 40-50 years of age, doubles every 10 years thereafter, and peaks at 75-80 years.
Besides colorectal cancer, other causes of blood in stool includes

   A. hemorrhoids
   B. fissures
   C. vascular ectasias
   D. all of the above

9. Within the field of geriatrics, there is an unusually-high probability that nurses will function in a multi-disciplinary approach in providing health care to patients, families and groups of elderly persons. Nurses who work in situations in which they must assume multidisciplinary functions need to

   A. be well-grounded as specialists in geriatrics and gerontology, in the knowledge of normal aging and in the areas of high-risk health problems among the elderly
   B. be visible to consumers, colleagues, and administrators in their nursing roles
   C. offer consultations and expect consultations and referrals on nursing problems
   D. all of the above

10. Persons at greater risk for adverse drug effects include all of the following EXCEPT those who are

    A. of extremely tall stature
    B. 75 years old or older
    C. receiving an excessive number of medications
    D. having renal dysfunction

11. The pharmacist will focus on the names and kinds of drugs being taken.
The nurse will look at some different dimensions, including

    A. previous patterns of utilization of medications
    B. attitudes towards medications and their effects, side effects, and allergies
    C. ethnic or religious influences on the treatment of illness and health maintenance
    D. all of the above

12. Barbiturates, benzodiazepines, and miscellaneous sedative and hypnotic agents comprise another group of drugs overused by the elderly.
    Barbiturates are to be avoided in the elderly because of all of the following risks, EXCEPT

    A. high potential for addiction
    B. hallucinations and delusions
    C. paradoxical agitation
    D. sedation and ataxia

13. Drugs such as chlorpromazine, thioridazine, haloperidol, and thiothixene are often overused by the elderly. Their continual use may cause

    A. extra-pyramidal symptoms such as drug-induced Parkinsonism
    B. tardive dyskinesia
    C. both of the above
    D. none of the above

14. Adequate nursing knowledge is one key to effectiveness in managing a medication regimen.
    For each drug, certain data is needed, but it is NOT necessary for the nurse to know

    A. the purpose of the medication, its function, and the disease or condition for which it is prescribed
    B. the generic and brand names of the medication, its color, and the size and shape of dosage form
    C. detailed information about the company who is manufacturing the drug
    D. the route of administration, e.g., by mouth, inhalation, intravenous, etc.

15. Which of the following questions should the nurse be able to answer for a discharging patient regarding the storage of a drug?

    A. Does the medication need to be refrigerated?
    B. Should it always be left in the original container?
    C. Does this medication have an especially short shelf life?
    D. All of the above

16. Professional health care providers, especially those providing nursing or rehabilitative patient care, should be competent enough in the practice of oral health maintenance to do all of the following EXCEPT

    A. perform gastric endoscopy routinely to rule out GI-related causes or bad oral health
    B. assess oral health status
    C. manage oral hygiene
    D. integrate oral health maintenance into patient care plan

17. A major responsibility in direct nursing care is to prevent progressive oral dysfunction syndrome.
    The classic and common example of PODS may be found in the institutionalized stroke patient who, after a year of post-stroke health care, displays all of the following characteristics EXCEPT

A. inability to cleanse mouth adequately caused by loss of motor skills for oral hygiene
B. inadequate control of dental plaque with rampant tooth decay and advanced periodontal disease
C. oral problems that are extremely resistant to drug treatment and keep on deteriorating
D. progressive loss of self-esteem due to poor esthetics and a noticeable offensive odor from the mouth

18. Dentures are not necessarily used to sustain life, although many patients will not eat appropriately or socialize when their teeth are out of their mouths. Common denture problems often managed by nursing intervention do NOT include 18.____

    A. mixed-up or lost dentures
    B. maintaining good hygiene of dentures to prevent caries or plaque
    C. ill-fitting dentures
    D. broken or poorly functioning dentures

19. Regarding oral health, the nurse who cares for an older person over a period of time should know the 19.____

    A. skills and resources employed to maintain oral health and those being avoided or used ineffectively
    B. patterns in lifestyle that are barriers to oral health, e.g., mouth care, lack of professional care, diet, fluids, and smoking
    C. planning and skills associated with patient's self-care of specific problems, such as protecting damaged or friable oral tissue, dry mouth, bad smell, and so forth
    D. locating resources for professional dental care needs

20. Nurses should routinely evaluate the effectiveness of the oral health practices being performed by persons in their charge. 20.____
    When a mouth has been cleansed daily over a period of time, it should have all of the following characteristics EXCEPT

    A. dental plaque should not be apparent on teeth
    B. tissues should be extremely smooth around the teeth
    C. patient should appreciate the feeling of a clean mouth
    D. there should be no bleeding when brushing or flossing

21. When dental personnel enter an institutional situation, they should 21.____

    A. write all findings, plans, and notes in the chart, with oral hygiene measures specifically written
    B. assist in the training and assessment of oral health maintenance
    C. both of the above
    D. none of the above

22. Each patient needs his own toothbrush, either hand or electric. 22.____
    A nurse should NOT recommend a toothbrush with

    A. curved handle and brushing surfaces
    B. soft nylon bristles
    C. bristle part small enough to reach all areas of mouth easily

D. straight handle and flat brushing surface

23. Recommended care of a toothbrush involves all of the following points EXCEPT: 23.____

   A. Rinse the toothbrush with clean, cold water, and use it to remove any retained food and toothpaste
   B. Store the toothbrush in a dark, airtight place
   C. Use an empty water glass or toothbrush holder to store the toothbrush
   D. Replace the toothbrush when the bristles become loose, bent, broken, or worn

24. Electric toothbrushes may be as effective as hand toothbrushes in maintaining cleanliness of the mouth. 24.____
   The recommended method of toothbrushing with an electric toothbrush is to

   A. wet the bristles of the toothbrush with water and place a small amount of dentifrice on them
   B. hold the bristles of the brush lightly against the side of the teeth so that both the teeth and gums are cleaned
   C. brush the tongue side as well as the cheek side of the teeth
   D. all of the above

KEY (CORRECT ANSWERS)

1.	D	11.	D
2.	A	12.	B
3.	C	13.	C
4.	B	14.	C
5.	B	15.	D
6.	D	16.	A
7.	C	17.	C
8.	D	18.	B
9.	D	19.	D
10.	A	20.	B

21. B
22. C
23. A
24. B
25. D

TEST 2

DIRECTIONS: Each question or incomplete statement is followed by several suggested answers or completions. Select the one that BEST answers the question or completes the statement. *PRINT THE LETTER OF THE CORRECT ANSWER IN THE SPACE AT THE RIGHT.*

1. Old people are susceptible to many of the diseases of younger adults. Studies of pattern of disease in the United States reveals that the major categories of diseases in elderly people require that special considerations include diseases

    A. that occur to varying degrees in all aged persons, such as atherosclerosis or cataracts
    B. with increased incidence in those of advanced age but not occurring universally, e.g., neoplastic disease, diabetes mellitus, and some dementing disorders
    C. that have more serious consequences in the elderly because of their reduced ability to maintain homeostasis, for example pneumonia, influenza, and trauma
    D. all of the above

    1.___

2. A screening profile of individuals at high risk for family mediated abuse or neglect includes all of the following elders EXCEPT those who

    A. live at home and whose needs exceed or soon will exceed their families' ability to meet them
    B. have primary caretakers who are expressing interest and sympathy in dealing with care needs
    C. live in families with a norm of family violence
    D. abuse drugs or alcohol or live with family members who abuse drugs or alcohol or have episodes of loss of control

    2.___

3. Constipation is known to occur in at least 25% of older patients, and many reasons have been cited as potentially influential.
NOT included among the factors believed to be contributory is

    A. increase in fluid intake
    B. lack of fiber in the diet to stimulate peristalsis
    C. blunting or loss of the defecation reflex as a consequence of neglect of the urge to defecate
    D. lack of exercise

    3.___

4. Oral health maintenance implies that the nurse provide

    A. daily oral hygiene as part of the total patient nursing care
    B. assessment of the mouth at intervals of time appropriate to the patient's health status and his ability to care for himself
    C. advocacy linkage to dental care when problems are detected
    D. all of the above

    4.___

5. For millions of Americans over age 65, osteoporosis is a debilitating disease that reduces their mobility and independence.
Factors thought to increase net bone losses of calcium include all of the following EXCEPT

    5.___

A. inadequate dietary intake of calcium and vitamin D
B. smoking and excessive alcohol and caffeine consumption
C. excessive physical activity
D. excessive dietary intake of phosphorus and proteins

6. Foods and fluids that aid in the prevention and management of constipation include   6.____

   A. raw vegetables and fruits
   B. at least 6 glasses of water per day
   C. whole grain cereal products
   D. all of the above

7. Suggested treatment and treatment combinations in a woman with post-menopausal   7.____
   osteoporosis include all of the following EXCEPT

   A. discourage exercise and advise complete bed rest
   B. assure an adequate supply of calcium and vitamin D plus sunlight exposure
   C. take anabolic steroids and estrogen/progestrin combinations as directed by physician
   D. supplement fluoride, especially in areas where water sources are low

8. The physiological, psychological, social, and economic changes that occur in aging people may result in a pattern of living which causes malnutrition and further physical and mental deterioration! for example, they   8.____

   A. cannot afford to do so
   B. have limited mobility which may impair their capacity to shop and cook for themselves
   C. have feelings of rejection and loneliness which obliterate the incentive necessary to prepare and eat a meal alone
   D. all of the above

9. If effective learning is to take place, the instructor must stimulate an interest in the subject of nutrition. It is NOT advisable for a person eating alone to   9.____

   A. set an attractive table, i.e., make meals an event
   B. never watch TV or listen to the radio while eating
   C. eat outdoors when the weather allows
   D. invite guests often for a potluck or meal exchange

10. Special facets of the federally supported nutrition demonstrating-research projects are   10.____
    basic to the success that many of these projects have appreciated.
    Among the supplemental provisions are

    A. auxiliary services, such as transportation, dental care, and counseling on individual dietary requirements to make it possible for older people to use services
    B. social settings designated for personal adjustment and adequacy of diet
    C. settings conducive to eating meals with others
    D. all of the above

11. Not all primary caregivers experience difficulties in their daily living associated with providing care to the elderly, dependent relatives in their families. Factors increasing the risk of problems in daily living include all of the following EXCEPT   11.____

A. lack of community resources
B. adequate income
C. environmental barriers, such as transportation and housing
D. substance abuse

12. When the demands on primary caregivers and other family members are seen to exceed their resources and disrupt their daily living, emotional responses normally occur. The nurse's role is to help family members

    A. recognize and accept their emotional responses to the situation
    B. accept their responses as abnormal and illegitimate
    C. both of the above
    D. none of the above

13. Restoration or maintenance of balance in a family may require an interdisciplinary team. It becomes important that one member of that team be identified as the coordinator responsible for the case management.
    This individual has a responsibility to

    A. coordinate services and conduct case conferences
    B. keep team members informed about the care plans
    C. conduct ongoing evaluations and updates of the evaluation plans
    D. all of the above

14. Delirium is a common condition, particularly in the hospital setting, and is most often a manifestation of serious systemic disease or an abnormal response to treatment. Diagnostic criteria of delirium includes all of the following EXCEPT

    A. clouding of consciousness
    B. loss of intellectual abilities of sufficient severity to interfere with social or occupational functioning
    C. clinical features that develop over a short period of time and tend to fluctuate over the course of the day
    D. disorientation and memory impairment

15. Dementias are actually a group of diseases sharing a gradual onset, global decline in intellectual capacity and performance, and progressive social incapacitation. The one of the following that is NOT a type of primary dementia is

    A. primary degenerative dementia (Alzheimer's disease)
    B. multi-infarct dementia
    C. Parkinson's dementia
    D. Pick's disease

16. Dementia is an ancient term taken from Latin and literally means *out of one's mind*. Diagnostic criteria for dementia include all of the following EXCEPT

    A. loss of intellectual abilities of sufficient severity to interfere with social or occupational functioning
    B. clouding of consciousness
    C. memory impairment
    D. impaired judgment

17. Nurses may feel some diagnostic confusion between delirium and dementia. Of the following, the feature that favors the diagnosis of dementia is:

    A. Onset of disease is rapid and duration of disease is hours to weeks
    B. Awareness is always impaired
    C. Course of disease is relatively stable
    D. Physical illness or drug toxicity is usually present

18. An older man is on MAO inhibitors for depressive disorder. The nurse should restrict all of the following foods to avoid hypertensive disorder EXCEPT

    A. old cheese
    B. chocolate
    C. white meat
    D. red wines

19. Agitation and restlessness are two of the most pressing behavioral problems that create difficulties in managing everyday living.
    Deterioration is LEAST likely to occur

    A. during periods of fatigue
    B. during early morning hours
    C. following ingestion of certain medications, e.g., indomethacin, pentazocin, and phenytoin, etc.
    D. when infections are present

20. Daily living is MOST likely to be compromised in the presence of agitation and restlessness when those around the agitated person

    A. cannot tolerate the behavior
    B. understand the phenomenon
    C. have workable strategies for dealing with situations
    D. all of the above

21. Manifestations of agitation and restlessness are wide-ranging in both form and severity, including all of the following EXCEPT

    A. long attention span
    B. constantly moving hands, e.g., picking at clothing, dressing and undressing, hand wringing, and twisting paper
    C. an inability to sit still, even for meals
    D. prowling aimlessly about neighborhood

22. Evidences that the everyday living of these agitated and restless elderly persons is not being managed effectively include

    A. exhaustion from lack of sleep or rest
    B. weight loss from burning more calories than they take time to eat
    C. being abused, assaulted, or robbed
    D. all of the above

23. Of the following, which is NOT a goal of nursing treatment plans for restless and agitated persons?

    A. Maintaining nutrition and elimination
    B. Arranging for adequate sleep and rest
    C. Providing a safe, completely isolated environment
    D. Providing for a more comfortable lifestyle

24. Older persons who are MORE likely to manage their current daily living by engaging in aggressive, hostile, and combative behavior are usually

    A. experiencing hearing or vision losses
    B. sharing living space with a person who has similar sensory deficits
    C. frustrated with self at being unable to do what was formerly possible
    D. all of the above

25. Factors that predict the likelihood of hostile, combative behavior continuing as an element in daily living include all of the following EXCEPT

    A. previous pattern of episodes of this behavior
    B. evidence of such behavior in the family
    C. nature of the events that triggers the behavior and the likelihood that such events will recur
    D. the nature of reinforcement the behavior has received

KEY (CORRECT ANSWERS)

1. D		11. B	
2. B		12. A	
3. A		13. D	
4. D		14. B	
5. C		15. C	
6. D		16. B	
7. A		17. C	
8. D		18. C	
9. B		19. B	
10. D		20. A	

21. A
22. D
23. C
24. D
25. B

EXAMINATION SECTION
TEST 1

DIRECTIONS: Each question or incomplete statement is followed by several suggested answers or completions. Select the one that BEST answers the question or completes the statement. *PRINT THE LETTER OF THE CORRECT ANSWER IN THE SPACE AT THE RIGHT.*

1. Multiphasic screening, now adopted by many health departments, is BEST defined as a

    A. new method of testing vision
    B. case finding procedure combining tests for several diseases
    C. combined vision and hearing test
    D. new method of cancer detection

2. Of the following statements that a nurse might make to a patient ill with cancer who says, *I don't think I'll ever get better. When the pain comes, I'm afraid I'll die before anyone gets here,* the one which would be MOST appropriate is:

    A. I wouldn't worry about that. People do not die because of pain.
    B. Of course you'll get better. You look much better than you did the last time I was here.
    C. You should try to have someone here with you and not be alone. Then you won't be afraid.
    D. I think I understand how you feel, but why do you think you won't get better?

3. In an epidemiological study of a disease, the one of the following steps which would usually NOT be included is

    A. collecting and compiling data on the incidence, prevalence, and trends of the disease
    B. reviewing the *natural history* of the disease
    C. making a sociological study of the community in which the disease is prevalent
    D. defining gaps in knowledge and developing hypotheses on which to base further investigation

4. Adequate lighting in the school is an important part of the sight conservation program. The school nurse familiar with standards for classroom lighting should know that the RECOMMENDED illumination on each desk for ordinary classroom work is _____ candles.

    A. 20-foot   B. 35-foot   C. 50-foot   D. 75-foot

5. The relation of fluorine to dental health has been the subject of extensive study for many years.
Of the following statements concerning the relation of fluorine to dental caries, the one which is CORRECT is that

    A. mass medication by fluorine is now accepted as the best means of treating and curing dental caries
    B. fluoridation of water supplies, though effective, is too expensive for wide usage
    C. fluoridation is effective only in children born in areas in which fluoridation exists
    D. fluoridation prevents dental caries but does not treat or cure it

6. There are measures which are effective in the prevention of diabetes in those with an hereditary disposition.
   Of the following, the one which has the GREATEST value as a preventive measure is

   A. preventing acute infection
   B. preventing obesity
   C. avoidance of emotional stress
   D. avoidance of marriage with a known diabetic

7. The basis of a program of *natural childbirth* is to

   A. prevent or dispel fear through education in the physiology of pregnancy
   B. reduce premature births and the complications of pregnancy
   C. reduce the maternal and neonatal mortality rates
   D. prepare the mother's body for the muscular activity of delivery

8. The one of the following statements which is CORRECT concerning retrolental fibroplasia is that it is a

   A. blood dyscrasia
   B. condition occurring in Rh negative infants whose mothers are Rh positive
   C. condition causing blindness in premature infants
   D. complication of congenital syphilis

9. Of the following factors, the one which is MOST important in maintaining optimum health in the older age group is

   A. regular medical supervision for early recognition and treatment of minor symptoms
   B. economic independence which gives a feeling of security
   C. avoidance of all emotional tensions
   D. adjustment of the environment to prevent physical and mental strain

10. The MOST outstanding result of antibiotic therapy in the treatment of syphilis has been to

    A. reduce the toxic effect of treatment
    B. shorten the treatment period
    C. prevent a relapse
    D. prevent late complications

11. To achieve the most effective and economical case finding for tuberculosis, mass examinations should be conducted PRIMARILY for

    A. infants under one year
    B. industrial workers
    C. elementary school students
    D. pre-school age group

12. Though tuberculosis occurs in all age groups, there is a certain period of life when individuals have the greatest resistance to the infection.
    That period is

    A. under one year of age
    B. between 3 years and puberty
    C. between 15 and 35 years of age
    D. between 25 and 40 years of age

13. Drug therapy for tuberculosis has proven to be an important tool in the control of the disease in its active stage.
    Of the following, the one which has had the MOST satisfactory results to date in that fewer patients develop resistance to the drug and the incidence of drug toxicity is reduced is

    A. para-amino-salicylic acid (P.A.S.) in combination with streptomycin
    B. dihydro-streptomycin
    C. streptomycin in combination with promine
    D. penicillin

13.____

14. Studies have indicated that the use of streptomycin in the treatment of tuberculosis has GREATEST value in

    A. recently developed pneumonic or exudative lesions
    B. long standing infections which have been resistant to other therapies
    C. military T.B.
    D. meningeal T.B.

14.____

15. The PARTICULAR effectiveness of chemotherapeutic agents in the treatment of pulmonary tuberculosis is that they

    A. are important adjuncts to surgery
    B. inhibit the growth of the bacillus
    C. heal lesions rapidly
    D. render the patient non-infectious

15.____

KEY (CORRECT ANSWERS)

1. B
2. D
3. C
4. A
5. D

6. B
7. A
8. C
9. A
10. B

11. B
12. B
13. A
14. A
15. B

TEST 2

DIRECTIONS: Each question or incomplete statement is followed by several suggested answers or completions. Select the one that BEST answers the question or completes the statement. *PRINT THE LETTER OF THE CORRECT ANSWER IN THE SPACE AT THE RIGHT.*

1. The CHIEF shortcoming of chemotherapeutic agents in the treatment of pulmonary tuberculosis is

    A. their prohibitive cost in any long-term treatment
    B. the toxic effects which follow their use
    C. that their use is limited to early cases
    D. the development of bacterial resistance by the host

    1.____

2. Though precise knowledge concerning the optimum duration of chemotherapy in treating pulmonary tuberculosis is lacking, the present APPROVED practice is

    A. continued uninterrupted treatment until the sputum is negative
    B. short courses of treatment with rest periods in between
    C. continued treatment for a minimum of 12 months
    D. continued treatment for one year after a negative sputum and cultures are obtained

    2.____

3. A community program for the control of tuberculosis must include school children and school personnel if it is to be a success.
   Of the following statements, the one which BEST represents expert opinion on the use of B.C.G. vaccine in the school program for tuberculosis control is that

    A. through immunization of all school children it serves as an important control measure
    B. its chief value is that it is an inexpensive and rapid method of case finding
    C. it would nullify the subsequent use of the tuberculin test which is the best case finding method for schools
    D. it is a valuable diagnostic method which would reduce the evidence of contact with active cases

    3.____

4. Nutritional deficiencies are a common problem in geriatrics.
   The dietary adjustment usually necessary to maintain PROPER nutrition for the average person in the older age group is

    A. increased proteins and vitamins
    B. elimination of fats
    C. increased carbohydrates
    D. elimination of roughage

    4.____

5. The death rate from cancer can be reduced by early diagnosis and treatment. It is important, therefore, for the nurse to assist in case finding.
   She should know that, of the following sites, the one which the GREATEST incidence of cancer in women occurs is the

    A. mouth   B. skin   C. breast   D. rectum

    5.____

6. Many cancers appear to develop when pre-existing abnormal conditions and changes in the tissue are present.
   Of the following, the one which is at present considered PRECANCEROUS is

   A. fibroid tumor
   B. chronic cervicitis
   C. fat tissue tumor
   D. sebaceous cyst

7. The diagnosis of cancer by examination of isolated cells in body secretions is known as

   A. biopsy
   B. aspiration technique
   C. histological diagnosis
   D. Papanicolaou smear

8. Of the following statements concerning our present knowledge of the etiology of human cancer, the one which is TRUE is that

   A. there is definite evidence that some cancers are caused by a virus
   B. some types of cancer are definitely contagious
   C. there is a strong possibility that cancer is transmitted from mother to baby in utero
   D. so many factors are involved that the discovery of a single cause is unlikely

9. The National Venereal Disease Control Program carried on by the Public Health Service of the U.S. Government is concerned PRIMARILY with

   A. promoting medical programs to provide early effective treatment of infected individuals
   B. a national program of education in the prevention of venereal diseases
   C. distribution of free drugs to physicians for the treatment of venereal disease
   D. providing funds for the education of physicians and nurses in the treatment and care of venereal disease

10. Of the following, the one which is of GREATEST importance in the prevention of poliomyelitis is to

    A. build up resistance with proper diet
    B. keep away from crowds during periods when the disease is prevalent
    C. immunize with gamma globulin
    D. adopt general public health measures for the protection of food and water

11. Of the following statements concerning the present status of chemotherapy in the treatment of cancer, the one which is TRUE is:

    A. Results to date indicate it may soon surpass radiation and surgery as an effective cure
    B. It has not proven effective except in cases where early diagnosis was made
    C. It must be used in conjunction with radiation or surgery
    D. It inhibits the growth of certain types of cancer and prolongs life but is not effective as a cure

12. The W.H.O. Regional Organization for Europe has set up a long-term plan for European health needs.
    Of the following activities, the one which is NOT planned as a major activity is

A. coordinating health policies in European countries
B. promoting improved service through demonstration of an ideal health program in one country
C. promoting professional and technical education for health workers in the member countries
D. providing for exchange of services among member nations

13. A health problem becomes the concern of public health authorities when the incidence is great and the mortality rate high.
In terms of this statement, of the following problems, the one which should be a PRIMARY concern is

   A. venereal diseases in young adults
   B. tuberculosis
   C. tropical diseases among ex-servicemen and their families
   D. degenerative diseases of middle and later life

14. Of the following, the one which is now considered to be the MOST common mode of transmission of poliomyelitis is

   A. infected insects
   B. contaminated water
   C. personal contact
   D. infected food

15. The incubation period for infantile paralysis is

   A. usually 7 to 14 days, but may vary from 3 to 35 days
   B. not known
   C. one week
   D. usually 48 hours, but may vary from 1 to 7 days

KEY (CORRECT ANSWERS)

1. D
2. C
3. C
4. A
5. C

6. B
7. D
8. D
9. A
10. B

11. D
12. B
13. D
14. C
15. A

EXAMINATION SECTION
TEST 1

DIRECTIONS: Each question or incomplete statement is followed by several suggested answers or completions. Select the one that BEST answers the question or completes the statement. *PRINT THE LETTER OF THE CORRECT ANSWER IN THE SPACE AT THE RIGHT.*

Questions 1-15.

DIRECTIONS: In the following questions numbered 1 through 15, the word in capitals is the name of an anatomical part which is a segment of a larger structure or system For each question, select the letter preceding the structure or system of which the word in capitals is a part.

1. ESOPHAGUS
    A. circulatory system
    B. bronchi
    C. submaxillary
    D. respiratory system

2. ALVEOLI
    A. nervous system
    B. lungs
    C. endocrine system
    D. muscle

3. DELTOID
    A. upper arm
    B. rib cage
    C. circulatory system
    D. superior vena cava

4. FEMORAL ARTERY
    A. right ventricle
    B. left auricle
    C. circulatory system
    D. lymphatic system

5. BRACKIAL PLEXUS
    A. circulatory system
    B. nervous system
    C. respiratory system
    D. bronchi

6. ERYTHROCYTE
    A. lymph glands
    B. skeletal system
    C. blood
    D. large intestine

7. STERNUM
    A. spinal column
    B. muscular system
    C. nervous system
    D. skeletal system

8. THYMUS
    A. endocrine system
    B. pituitary gland
    C. parathyroids
    D. adrenals

9. MANDIBLE
    A. pelvis   B. head   C. liver   D. stomach

83

10. PECTORAL

　　A. skeletal system　　　　B. patella
　　C. chest　　　　　　　　　D. digestive tract

11. CORNEA

　　A. arm　　B. eye　　C. blood　　D. lymph

12. CRANIUM

　　A. circulatory system　　B. left auricle
　　C. skeletal system　　　　D. abdomen

13. TRAPEZIUS

　　A. breastbone　　　　B. muscular system
　　C. endocrine system　D. spinal column

14. MEGALOBLAST

　　A. blood　　B. pelvis　　C. spleen　　D. head

15. ADRENAL

　　A. mouth　　　B. respiratory system
　　C. liver　　　D. endocrine system

Questions 16-25.

DIRECTIONS: The following questions numbered 16 through 25 are concerned with various categories of diseases. For each question, select the letter preceding the disease or condition which MOST properly belongs to the category listed.

16. BONE DISEASE

　　A. arrhythmia　　B. arthritis
　　C. edema　　　　　D. gastritis

17. DISEASE OF THE DIGESTIVE SYSTEM

　　A. diabetes　　B. osteomyelitis
　　C. ileitis　　 D. conjunctivitis

18. DISEASE OF THE RESPIRATORY SYSTEM

　　A. cyanosis　　B. poliomyelitis
　　C. jaundice　　D. bronchiectasis

19. DISEASE OF THE HEART

　　A. hepatitis　　　B. influenza
　　C. encephalitis　 D. myocarditis

20. DISEASE OF THE BLOOD

　　A. leukemia　　B. diphtheria
　　C. pneumonia　 D. colitis

21. NUTRITIONAL DISEASE   21._____

    A. hyperemia   B. mononucleosis
    C. trichinosis   D. scurvy

22. DISEASE OF THE NERVOUS SYSTEM   22._____

    A. amebiasis   B. parkinsonism
    C. ascariasis   D. tapeworm

23. PARASITIC DISEASE   23._____

    A. salmonella   B. neuralgia
    C. hemophilia   D. bursitis

24. SKIN DISEASE   24._____

    A. hydrocephalus   B. leprosy
    C. adenitis   D. angina

25. DISEASE OF THE URINARY TRACT   25._____

    A. myasthenia gravis   B. colitis
    C. hydronephrosis   D. dermatitis

KEY (CORRECT ANSWERS)

1.	D	11.	B
2.	B	12.	C
3.	A	13.	B
4.	C	14.	A
5.	B	15.	D
6.	C	16.	B
7.	D	17.	C
8.	A	18.	D
9.	B	19.	D
10.	C	20.	A

21.	D
22.	B
23.	A
24.	B
25.	C

TEST 2

DIRECTIONS: Each question or incomplete statement is followed by several suggested answers or completions. Select the one that BEST answers the question or completes the statement. *PRINT THE LETTER OF THE CORRECT ANSWER IN THE SPACE AT THE RIGHT.*

Questions 1-10.

DIRECTIONS: Questions 1 through 10 are concerned with various categories of diseases. For each question, select the letter preceding the disease or condition which MOST properly belongs to the category listed.

1. DISEASE OF THE HEART

    A. diabetes B. tachycardia
    C. osteoporosis D. adenitis

2. SKIN DISEASE

    A. cholelithiasis B. colitis
    C. psoriasis D. encephalitis

3. DISEASE OF THE BLOOD

    A. polycythemia B. ileitis
    C. psoitis D. dermatitis

4. DISEASE OF THE RESPIRATORY SYSTEM

    A. dysentery B. angina
    C. hemophilia D. pneumonia

5. DISEASE OF THE DIGESTIVE SYSTEM

    A. periastitis B. bronchiectasis
    C. enteritis D. pertussis

6. PARASITIC DISEASE

    A. ascariasis B. nephritis
    C. hyperemia D. neuralgia

7. NUTRITIONAL DISEASE

    A. entasis B. pellagra
    C. amebiasis D. diphtheria

8. BONE DISEASE

    A. gangrene B. epilepsy
    C. osteochondritis D. bronchitis

9. DISEASE OF THE NERVOUS SYSTEM

    A. mononucleosis B. gallstones
    C. jaundice D. multiple sclerosis

10. DISEASE OF THE URINARY TRACT 10.____

    A. hydrocephalus   B. glomerulonephritis
    C. cyanosis   D. bursitis

Questions 11-25.

DIRECTIONS: For the following questions 11 through 25, select the letter preceding the part or system of the body which is CHIEFLY affected by the disease in capitals.

11. CONJUNCTIVITIS 11.____

    A. ear   B. intestines
    C. eye   D. liver

12. EMPHYSEMA 12.____

    A. heart   B. bronchial tubes
    C. pancreas   D. lymph nodes

13. CHOLELITHIASIS 13.____

    A. muscles   B. liver
    C. bones   D. common bile duct

14. PYELONEPHRITIS 14.____

    A. intestinal tract   B. arterial walls
    C. ligaments   D. urinary tract

15. EPILEPSY 15.____

    A. nervous system   B. pancreas
    C. thyroid   D. stomach

16. DYSENTERY 16.____

    A. tendons   B. kidneys
    C. intestines   D. brain

17. ERYTHROBLASTOSIS 17.____

    A. kidneys   B. blood
    C. endocrine system   D. large intestine

18. GLAUCOMA 18.____

    A. blood vessels   B. cortex
    C. cerebellum   D. eye

19. OSTEOPOROSIS 19.____

    A. bones   B. central nervous system
    C. adrenals   D. lymph nodes

20. MENINGITIS 20.____

    A. nasal passages   B. intestinal tract
    C. spinal cord   D. urinary tract

21. BURSITIS 21.____

    A. urinary tract   B. bones
    C. nasal passages   D. heart

22. ENDOCARDITIS 22.____

    A. cortex   B. kidneys   C. pancreas   D. heart

23. DIVERTICULOSIS 23.____

    A. thyroid   B. endocrine system
    C. intestinal tract   D. kidneys

24. ENCEPHALITIS 24.____

    A. brain   B. vessels   C. kidneys   D. eye

25. ILEITIS 25.____

    A. nervous system   B. blood
    C. liver   D. intestinal tract

KEY (CORRECT ANSWERS)

1.	B	11.	C
2.	C	12.	B
3.	A	13.	D
4.	D	14.	D
5.	C	15.	A
6.	A	16.	C
7.	B	17.	B
8.	C	18.	D
9.	D	19.	A
10.	B	20.	C

21. B
22. D
23. C
24. A
25. D

EXAMINATION SECTION
TEST 1

DIRECTIONS: Each question or incomplete statement is followed by several suggested answers or completions. Select the one that BEST answers the question or completes the statement. *PRINT THE LETTER OF THE CORRECT ANSWER IN THE SPACE AT THE RIGHT.*

Questions 1-20.

DIRECTIONS: Column I below lists words used in medical practice. Column II lists phrases which describe the words in Column I. Opposite the number preceding each of the words in Column I, place the letter preceding the phrase in Column II which BEST describes the word in Column I.

COLUMN I

1. Abrasion
2. Aseptic
3. Cardiac
4. Catarrh
5. Contamination
6. Dermatology
7. Disinfectant
8. Dyspepsia
9. Epidemic
10. Epidermis
11. Incubation
12. Microscope
13. Pediatrics
14. Plasma
15. Prenatal
16. Retina
17. Syphilis
18. Syringe
19. Toxemia
20. Vaccine

COLUMN II

A. A disturbance of digestion
B. Destroying the germs of disease
C. A general poisoning of the blood
D. An instrument used for injecting fluids
E. A scraping off of the skin
F. Free from disease germs
G. An apparatus for viewing internal organs by means of x-rays
H. An instrument for assisting the eye in observing minute objects
I. An inoculable immunizing agent
J. The extensive prevalence in a community of a
K. Chemical product of an organ
L. Preceding birth
M. Fever
N. The branch of medical science that relates to the skin and its diseases
O. Fluid part of the blood
P. The science of the hygienic care of children
Q. Infection by contact
R. Relating to the heart
S. Inner structure of the eye
T. Outer portion of the skin
U. Pertaining to the ductless glands
V. An infectious venereal disease
W. The development of an infectious disease from the period of infection to that of the appearance of the first symptoms
X. Simple inflammation of a mucous membrane
Y. An instrument for measuring blood pressure

Questions 21-25.

DIRECTIONS: Each of Questions 21 through 25 consists of four words. Three of these words belong together. One word does NOT belong with the other three. For each group of words, you are to select the one word which does NOT belong with the other three words.

21.	A. conclude	B. terminate	C. initiate	D. end	21.___
22.	A. deficient C. excessive		B. inadequate D. insufficient		22.___
23.	A. rare	B. unique	C. unusual	D. frequent	23.___
24.	A. unquestionable C. doubtful		B. uncertain D. indefinite		24.___
25.	A. stretch	B. contract	C. extend	D. expand	25.___

KEY (CORRECT ANSWERS)

1. E
2. F
3. R
4. X
5. Q
6. N
7. B
8. A
9. J
10. T

11. W
12. H
13. P
14. O
15. L
16. S
17. V
18. D
19. C
20. I

21. C
22. C
23. D
24. A
25. B

TEST 2

DIRECTIONS: Each question or incomplete statement is followed by several suggested answers or completions. Select the one that BEST answers the question or completes the statement. *PRINT THE LETTER OF THE CORRECT ANSWER IN THE SPACE AT THE RIGHT.*

Questions 1-4.

DIRECTIONS: Questions 1 through 4 pertain to the meaning of terms which may be encountered in laboratory work. For each question, select the option whose meaning is MOST NEARLY the same as that of the numbered item.

1. Atrophied
    - A. enlarged
    - B. relaxed
    - C. strengthened
    - D. wasted

2. Leucocyte
    - A. white cell
    - B. red cell
    - C. epithelial cell
    - D. dermal cell

3. Permeable
    - A. volatile
    - B. variable
    - C. flexible
    - D. penetrable

4. Attenuate
    - A. dilute
    - B. infect
    - C. oxidize
    - D. strengthen

Questions 5-11.

DIRECTIONS: For Questions 5 through 11, select the letter preceding the word which means MOST NEARLY the same as the first word.

5. legible
    - A. readable
    - B. eligible
    - C. learned
    - D. lawful

6. observe
    - A. assist
    - B. watch
    - C. correct
    - D. oppose

7. habitual
    - A. punctual
    - B. occasional
    - C. usual
    - D. actual

8. chronological
    - A. successive
    - B. earlier
    - C. later
    - D. studious

9. arrest
   A. punish   B. run   C. threaten   D. stop

10. abstain
    A. refrain   B. indulge   C. discolor   D. spoil

11. toxic
    A. poisonous   B. decaying
    C. taxing   D. defective

12. The *initial* contact is of great importance in setting a pattern for future relations.
    The word *initial*, as used in this sentence, means MOST NEARLY
    A. first   B. written   C. direct   D. hidden

13. The doctor prescribed a diet which was *adequate* for the patient's needs.
    The word *adequate*, as used in this sentence, means MOST NEARLY
    A. insufficient   B. unusual
    C. required   D. enough

14. The child was reported to be suffering from a vitamin *deficiency*.
    The word *deficiency*, as used in this sentence, means MOST NEARLY
    A. surplus   B. infection   C. shortage   D. injury

15. In obtaining medical case data, a medical record librarian should discourage the patient from giving *irrelevant* information.
    The word *irrelevant*, as used in this sentence, means MOST NEARLY
    A. too detailed   B. pertaining to relatives
    C. insufficient   D. inappropriate

16. The doctor requested that a *tentative* appointment be made for the patient.
    The word *tentative*, as used in this sentence, means MOST NEARLY
    A. definite   B. subject to change
    C. later   D. of short duration

17. The black plague resulted in an usually high *mortality rate* in the population of Europe.
    The term *mortality rate*, as used in this sentence, means MOST NEARLY
    A. future immunity of the people
    B. death rate
    C. general weakening of the health of the people
    D. sickness rate

18. The public health assistant was asked to file a number of *identical* reports on the case.
    The word *identical*, as used in this sentence, means MOST NEARLY
    A. accurate   B. detailed   C. same   D. different

19. The nurse assisted in *the biopsy* of the patient.
    The word *biopsy*, as used in this sentence, means MOST NEARLY

    A. autopsy
    B. excision and diagnostic study of tissue
    C. biography and health history
    D. administering of anesthesia

    19._____

20. The assistant noted that the swelling on the patient's face had *subsided*.
    The word *subsided*, as used in this sentence, means MOST NEARLY

    A. become aggravated   B. increased
    C. vanished   D. abated

    20._____

21. The patient was given food *intravenously*.
    The word *intravenously*, as used in this sentence, means MOST NEARLY

    A. orally   B. against his will
    C. through the veins   D. without condiment

    21._____

Questions 22-25.

DIRECTIONS: Each of Questions 22 through 25 consists of four words. Three of these words belong together. One word does NOT belong with the other three. For each group of words, you are to select the one word which does NOT belong with the other three words.

22.	A.	accelerate	B.	quicken	C.	accept	D.	hasten	22._____
23.	A.	sever	B.	rupture	C.	rectify	D.	tear	23._____
24.	A.	innocuous	B.	injurious	C.	dangerous	D.	harmful	24._____
25.	A.	adulterate			B.	contaminate			25._____
	C.	taint			D.	disinfect			

KEY (CORRECT ANSWERS)

1.	D	11.	A	21.	C
2.	A	12.	A	22.	C
3.	D	13.	D	23.	C
4.	A	14.	C	24.	A
5.	A	15.	D	25.	D
6.	B	16.	B		
7.	C	17.	B		
8.	A	18.	C		
9.	D	19.	B		
10.	A	20.	D		

TEST 3

DIRECTIONS: Each question or incomplete statement is followed by several suggested answers or completions. Select the one that BEST answers the question or completes the statement. *PRINT THE LETTER OF THE CORRECT ANSWER IN THE SPACE AT THE RIGHT.*

Questions 1-25.

DIRECTIONS: Each of Questions 1 through 25 consists of a word, in capitals, followed by four suggested meanings of the word. For each question, indicate in the space at the right the letter preceding the word which means MOST NEARLY the same as the word in capitals.

1. TEMPORARY
    - A. permanently
    - B. for a limited time
    - C. at the same time
    - D. frequently

    1.____

2. INQUIRE
    - A. order
    - B. agree
    - C. ask
    - D. discharge

    2.____

3. SUFFICIENT
    - A. enough
    - B. inadequate
    - C. thorough
    - D. capable

    3.____

4. AMBULATORY
    - A. bedridden
    - B. left-handed
    - C. walking
    - D. laboratory

    4.____

5. DILATE
    - A. enlarge
    - B. contract
    - C. revise
    - D. restrict

    5.____

6. NUTRITIOUS
    - A. protective
    - B. healthful
    - C. fattening
    - D. nourishing

    6.____

7. CONGENITAL
    - A. with pleasure
    - B. defective
    - C. likeable
    - D. existing from birth

    7.____

8. ISOLATION
    - A. sanitation
    - B. quarantine
    - C. rudeness
    - D. exposure

    8.____

9. SPASM
    - A. splash
    - B. twitch
    - C. space
    - D. blow

    9.____

94

10. HEMORRHAGE
    A. bleeding
    B. ulcer
    C. hereditary disease
    D. lack of blood

11. NOXIOUS
    A. gaseous B. harmful C. soothing D. repulsive

12. PYOGENIC
    A. disease producing
    B. fever producing
    C. pus forming
    D. water forming

13. RENAL
    A. brain B. heart C. kidney D. stomach

14. ENDEMIC
    A. epidemic
    B. endermic
    C. endoblast
    D. peculiar to a particular people or locality, as a disease

15. MACULATION
    A. reticulation
    B. inoculation
    C. maturation
    D. defilement

16. TOLERATE
    A. fear B. forgive C. allow D. despise

17. VENTILATE
    A. vacate B. air C. extricate D. heat

18. SUPERIOR
    A. perfect
    B. subordinate
    C. lower
    D. higher

19. EXTREMITY
    A. extent B. limb C. illness D. execution

20. DIVULGED
    A. unrefined B. secreted C. revealed D. divided

21. SIPHON
    A. drain B. drink C. compute D. discard

22. EXPIRATION
    A. trip
    B. demonstration
    C. examination
    D. end

23. AEROSOL 23.____

    A. a gas dispersed in a liquid
    B. a liquid dispersed in a gas
    C. a liquid dispersed in a solid
    D. a solid dispersed in a liquid

24. ETIOLOGY 24.____

    A. cause of a disease   B. method of cure
    C. method of diagnosis   D. study of insects

25. IN VITRO 25.____

    A. in alkali   B. in the body
    C. in the test tube   D. in vacuum

KEY (CORRECT ANSWERS)

1.	B	11.	B
2.	C	12.	C
3.	A	13.	C
4.	C	14.	D
5.	A	15.	D
6.	D	16.	C
7.	D	17.	B
8.	B	18.	D
9.	B	19.	B
10.	A	20.	C

21. A
22. D
23. B
24. A
25. C

BASIC NURSING PROCEDURES: FUNDAMENTAL NURSING CARE OF THE PATIENT

TABLE OF CONTENTS

		Page
1.	Morning Care	1
2.	Oral Hygiene	2
3.	Special Mouth Care	3
4.	Care of Dentures	5
5.	Bed Bath	6
6.	Making an Unoccupied Bed	8
7.	Making an Occupied Bed	12
8.	Serving Diets from Food Cart	16
9.	Central Tray Service	18
10.	Care of Ice Machine and Handling of Ice, Bedside Pitchers and Glasses	19
11.	Feeding the Helpless Patient	21
12.	Evening Care	22
13.	Care of the Seriously Ill Patient	23

BASIC NURSING PROCEDURES: FUNDAMENTAL NURSING CARE OF THE PATIENT

1. MORNING CARE

PURPOSE

To refresh and prepare patient for breakfast.

EQUIPMENT

Basin of warm water
Towel, washcloth and soap
Toothbrush and dentifrice/mouthwash
Curved basin
Glass of water
Comb

PROCEDURE

1. Clear bedside stand or overbed table for food tray.
2. Offer bedpan and urinal.
3. Wash patient's face and hands.
4. Give oral hygiene.
5. Place patient in a comfortable position for breakfast.
6. Comb hair.

POINTS TO EMPHASIZE

1. Morning care is given before breakfast by night corpsman.
2. Assist handicapped, aged or patients on complete bed rest.

CARE OF EQUIPMENT

Wash, dry and replace equipment.

2. ORAL HYGIENE

PURPOSE

To keep mouth clean.
To refresh patient.
To prevent infection and complications in the oral cavity.
To stimulate appetite.

EQUIPMENT

Glass of water
Curved basin
Toothbrush and dentifrice - electric toothbrush if available
Mouth wash
Towel
Drinking tubes as necessary

PROCEDURE

1. A patient who is able to help himself:
   a. Place patient in comfortable position.
   b. Arrange equipment on bedside table within his reach.

2. A patient who needs assistance:
   a. Place patient in comfortable position.
   b. Place towel under his chin and over bedding.
   c. Moisten brush, apply dentifrice and hand to the patient.
   d. Hold curved basin under his chin while he cleanses his teeth and mouth.
   e. Remove basin. Wipe lips and chin with towel.

POINTS TO EMPHASIZE

Oral hygiene is particularly important for patients
   a. who are not taking food and fluid by mouth
   b. with nasogastric tubes
   c. with productive coughs
   d. who are receiving oxygen therapy

CARE OF EQUIPMENT

Wash equipment with soap and hot water, rinse, dry and put away.

3. SPECIAL MOUTH CARE

PURPOSE

To cleanse and refresh mouth.
To prevent infection.

EQUIPMENT

Electric toothbrush if available
Tray with:
- Mineral oil or cold cream
- Lemon-glycerine applicators
- Paper bag
- Drinking tubes or straws
- Applicators and gauze sponges
- Curved basin
- Paper wipes
- Bulb syringe

Cleansing agents

- Tooth paste
- Equal parts of hydrogen peroxide and water
- Mouthwash

Glass of water
Suction machine for unconscious patient

PROCEDURE

1. Tell patient what you are going to do.
2. Turn patient's head to one side.
3. Brush teeth and gums.
4. When it is not possible to brush teeth and gums, moisten applicator with a cleansing agent and use for cleaning oral cavity and teeth.
5. Assist patient to rinse mouth with water.
6. If patient is unable to use drinking tube, gently irrigate the mouth with a syringe directing the flow of water to side of mouth.
7. Apply lubricant to lips.

For Unconscious Patient

Use suction machine.

SPECIAL MOUTH CARE (Continued)

POINTS TO EMPHASIZE
1. Extreme care should be exercised to prevent injury to the gums.
2. Position patient carefully to prevent aspiration of fluids.
3. Caution patient not to swallow mouthwash.

CARE OF EQUIPMENT

Dispose of applicator and soiled gauze. Clean equipment and restock tray.

4. CARE OF DENTURES

PURPOSE

To aid in keeping mouth in good condition.
To cleanse the teeth.

EQUIPMENT

Container for dentures
Toothbrush and dentifrice
Glass of water
Mouthwash
Curved basin
Towel
Paper towels

PROCEDURE

1. Have patient rinse mouth with mouthwash.
2. Remove dentures. Place them in container.
3. Have patient brush tongue and gums with mouth-wash.
4. Place a basin under tap in sink and place paper towels in basin. Fill basin with cold water.
5. Hold dentures over basin and under cold running water. Wash with brush and dentifrice.
6. Place dentures in container of cold water. Take to patient's bedside.
7. Replace wet dentures.

POINTS TO EMPHASIZE

1. Handle dentures carefully to prevent breakage.
2. When not in use, dentures should be placed in covered container of cold water and placed in top drawer of locker.
3. Give special attention to the inner surfaces of clips used to hold bridge work or partial plates in place.

CARE OF EQUIPMENT

Wash equipment, rinse, dry and put away.

5. BED BATH

PURPOSE

To cleanse the skin.
To stimulate the circulation.
To observe the patient mentally and physically.
To aid in elimination.

EQUIPMENT

Linen and pajamas as required
Half filled basin of water
Bar of soap
Rubbing alcohol/skin lotion
Bedpan and urinal with cover
Bed screens

PROCEDURE

1. Tell patient what you are going to do.
2. Screen patient.
3. Offer bedpan and urinal.
4. Shave patient or allow patient to shave himself.
5. Lower backrest and knee rest if physical condition permits.
6. Loosen top bedding at foot and sides of bed.
7. Remove pillow and place on chair.
8. Remove and fold bedspread and blanket. Place on back of chair.
9. Remove pajamas and place on chair.
10. Assist patient to near side of bed.
11. Bathe the patient:

    a. Eyes:
       (1) Do not use soap.
       (2) Clean from inner to outer corner of eye.

    b. Face, neck and ears.
    c. Far arm.
    d. Place hand in basin and clean nails.
    e. Near arm.
    f. Place hand in basin and clean nails.
    g. Chest.
    h. Abdomen.

BED BATH (Continued)

PROCEDURE (Continued)

12.
- i. Far leg, foot and nails. Place foot in basin when possible.
- j. Near leg, foot and nails. Place foot in basin when possible.
- k. Change water. l. Back and buttocks.
- m. Genitals and rectal area.

13. Give back rub.
14. Put on pajamas.
15. Comb hair.
16. Make bed.
17. Adjust bed to patient's comfort unless contrain-dicated.

POINTS TO EMPHASIZE

1. Give bed baths daily and P.R.N.
2. Give oral hygiene before bath.
3. Avoid drafts which might cause chilling.
4. Use bath towel under all parts to aid in keeping the bed linen as dry as possible.
5. Change bath water after washing lower extremities and as necessary.
6. Be sure all soap film is rinsed from body to prevent skin irritation.
7. Keep patient well draped at all times.
8. Observe and chart the condition of the skin in regard to lesions, rashes and reddened areas.
9. Pillow should be removed unless contraindicated to give patient a change of position.
10. Assist handicapped patients with shaving.
11. Always move or turn patient toward you.

CARE OF EQUIPMENT

1. Remove soiled linen and place in hamper.
2. Wash equipment, rinse, dry and put away.

6. MAKING AN UNOCCUPIED BED

PURPOSE

To provide a clean, comfortable bed.
To provide a neat appearance to the ward.

EQUIPMENT

Two sheets
Plastic mattress cover
Blanket
Plastic pillow cover
Pillowcase
Protective draw sheet or disposable pads, if indicated

PROCEDURE

1. Place mattress cover on mattress. Where necessary and available, plastic mattress covers are used.
2. Place center fold of sheet in center of bed, narrow hem even with foot of bed.
3. Fold excess sheet under the mattress at head of bed.
4. Miter corner.
    a. Pick up hanging sheet 12 inches from head of bed.
    b. Tuck lower corner under mattress.
    c. Bring triangle down over side of bed.
    d. Tuck sheet under mattress.
5. Pull bottom sheet tight and tuck under side of mattress.
6. If draw sheets are indicated, place in center of bed as illustrated. Tuck excess under mattress.
    a. Linen draw sheet is made by folding a regular bed sheet in half - hem to hem.
7. Place center fold of second sheet in center of bed, with hem even with the top of mattress.
8. Tuck excess under foot of mattress.
9. Center fold blanket in middle of bed 6 inches from top of mattress.
10. Fold excess under foot of mattress.
11. Make mitered corner.

MAKING AN UNOCCUPIED BED (Continued)

PROCEDURE (Continued)

12. Place bedspread on bed, center fold in middle of bed even with the top of the mattress. Fold under blanket.
13. Fold cuff of top sheet over bedspread at head of bed.
14. Tuck excess spread under foot of mattress.
15. Miter corner at foot of mattress.
16. Go to other side of bed and follow steps 3 to 15.
17. Place plastic cover on pillow.
18. Place pillow case on pillow.
19. Place pillow on bed with seams at head of bed, open end away from the entrance to the ward.

POINTS TO EMPHASIZE

1. Woolen blankets are to be used only when cotton blankets are not available.
2. Never use woolen blankets when oxygen therapy is in use.
3. Use protective draw sheet or protective pads when indicated.

MITERED CORNER

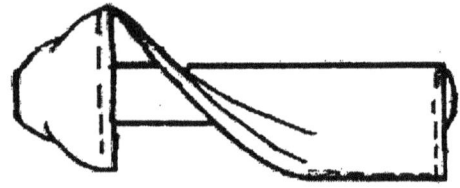

Pick up hanging sheet 12 inches from head of bed.

Tuck lower corner under mattress.

Bring triangle down over side of bed.

Tuck sheet under mattress.

COMPLETING FOUNDATION
APPLY DRAW SHEETS

1. PLACE RUBBER DRAW SHEET IN CENTER OF BED

2. TUCK EXCESS RUBBER DRAW SHEET IN ON NEAR SIDE OF MATTRESS

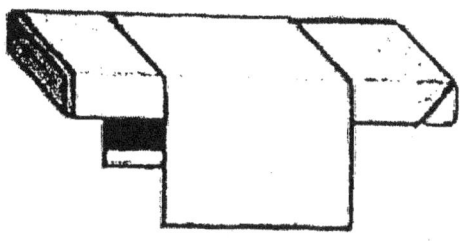

3. PLACE COTTON DRAW SHEET OVER RUBBER DRAW SHEET

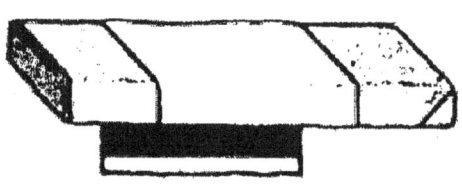

4. TUCK EXCESS COTTON DRAW SHEET IN ON NEAR SIDE OF MATTRESS

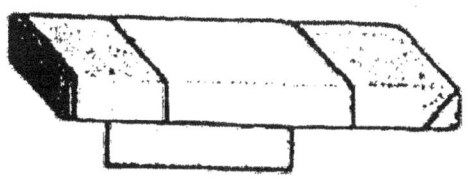

5. TUCK EXCESS RUBBER DRAW SHEET IN ON OPPOSITE SIDE OF MATTRESS

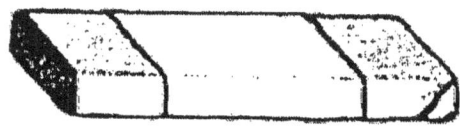

6. TUCK EXCESS COTTON DRAW SHEET IN ON OPPOSITE SIDE OF MATTRESS

7. MAKING AN OCCUPIED BED

PURPOSE

To provide clean linen with least exertion to patient.
To refresh patient.
To prevent pressure sores.

EQUIPMENT

Two sheets
Pillowcase
Blanket
Protective draw sheet or disposable pads, if indicated
Hamper

PROCEDURE

1. Place chair at foot of bed.
2. Push bedside locker away from bed.
3. Pull mattress to head of bed.
4. Loosen all bedding.
5. Remove pillow and place on chair.
6. Remove bedspread by folding from top to bottom, pick up in center and place on back of chair.
7. Remove blanket in same manner.
8. Turn patient to one side of the bed.
9. If cotton draw sheet is used, roll draw sheet close to patient's back.
10. Turn back protective sheet over patient.
11. Roll bottom sheet close to patient's back.
12. Straighten mattress cover as necessary.
13. Place clean sheet on bed with the center fold in the middle and narrow hem even with foot of bed.
14. Tuck in excess at head of bed. Miter corner and tuck in at side.
15. Bring down protective sheet; straighten and tuck in.
16. Make draw sheet by folding a sheet from hem to hem with smooth side out.
17. Place on bed with fold toward head of bed. Tuck in.

MAKING AN OCCUPIED BED (Continued)

PROCEDURE (Continued)

18. Roll patient over to completed side of bed.
19. Go to other side of the bed.
20. Remove soiled sheets and place in hamper.
21. Check soiled linen for personal articles.
22. Turn back draw sheets over patient.
23. Pull bottom sheet tight and smooth.
24. Pull protective sheet and draw sheet tight and smooth.
25. Bring patient to center of bed.
26. Place top sheet over patient, wide hem even with top of mattress.
27. Ask patient to hold clean top sheet.
28. Remove soiled top sheet. Place in hamper.
29. Place blanket 6 inches from top of mattress.
30. Make pleat in sheet and blanket over patient's toes.
31. Tuck in excess at foot of bed and miter corners.
32. Place bedspread on bed even with top of mattress. Fold under blanket.
33. Fold sheet over bedspread and blanket at head of bed.
34. Tuck in excess bedspread at foot of bed. Miter corners. Allow triangle to hang loosely.
35. Put clean pillowcase on pillow. Place under patient's head with closed end toward entrance to ward.
36. Adjust bed as desired by patient.
37. Straighten unit. Leave bedside stand within reach of patient.

POINTS TO EMPHASIZE

1. Always turn patient toward you to prevent possibility of injury and/or falls.
2. Make sure that foundation sheets are smooth and dry.

MAKING AN OCCUPIED BED

TURN PATIENT TOWARD YOU
FAN FOLD SOILED LINEN
AGAINST PATIENTS BACK

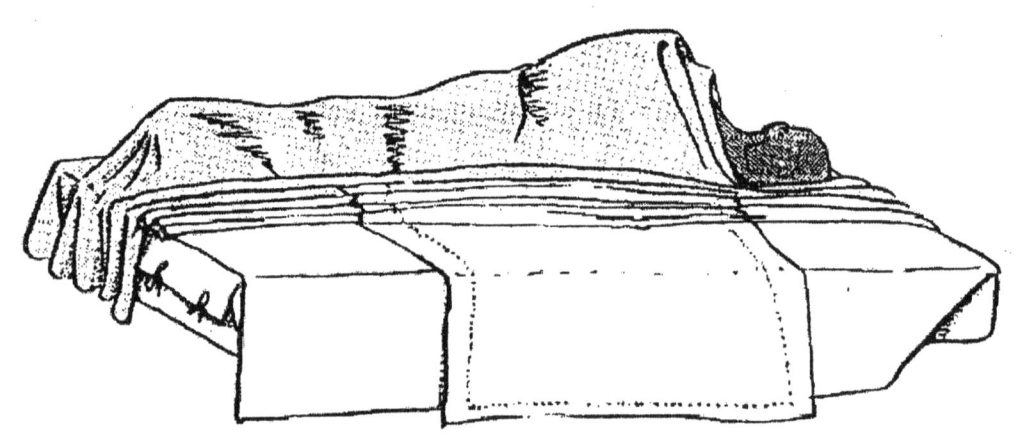

MAKE UP ONE HALF THE BED
BOTTOM SHEET, THEN
RUBBER DRAW SHEET

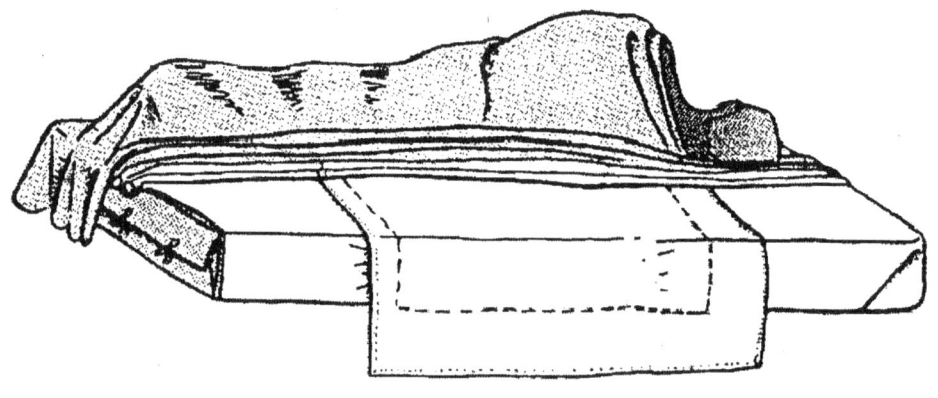

ADD COTTON DRAW SHEET

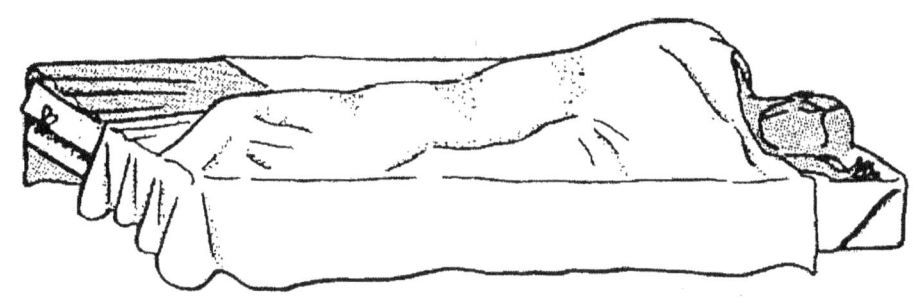

TURN PATIENT ONTO CLEAN LINEN
MAKE OPPOSITE SIDE OF BED

8. SERVING DIETS FROM FOOD CART

PURPOSE

To provide an attractively served food tray for a patient in a hospital where central food tray service is not available.

EQUIPMENT

Cart with food
Cart with trays, dishes, silver, and serving utensils

PROCEDURE

1. Clear the patient's bedside or overbed table.
2. Place table within patient's reach.
3. Place patient in a comfortable position.
4. Wash hands. Wheel food and tray carts to the unit.
5. Place beverage, salad, soup and dessert on the tray.
6. Fill glasses, cups and bowls three fourths full.
7. Serve small portions of hot food in an attractive manner.
8. Check diet list for type of diet each patient is to receive.
9. Carry tray and place it in a convenient position for the patient. Help the patient with the food if necessary.
10. After patient has finished, note how much he has eaten. Collect tray and return to main galley.

POINTS TO EMPHASIZE

1. The ward should be quiet and in readiness for meals.
2. Serve hot food hot and cold food cold.
3. Ice cream, sherbert and jello are kept in the refrigerator until ready to serve.
4. Do not hurry patient.
5. Do not smoke while working with food.
6. Refer to Special Diet Manual for special diet information.
7. Check visible file to determine if patient may have regular diet.
8. Make rounds to check that every patient has been served and received the correct diet.

SERVING DIETS FROM FOOD CART (Continued)

CARE OF EQUIPMENT WHERE MAIN GALLEY DOES NOT HAVE DISH WASHING FACILITIES

1. Scrape and stack dishes:
    a. Solid food into garbage can.
    b. Liquids into drain.
2. Clean and stack trays.
3. Wash dishes with hot soapy water. Stack in dish sterilizer.
4. Follow instructions on sterilizer. Temperature of final rinse water 180° F. Allow to air dry. Put away.
5. Place trays on cart with tray cover, silver and napkins. Salt, pepper, sugar go on all trays except Special Diets.
6. Clean food cart. Return to main galley.

9. CENTRAL TRAY SERVICE

PURPOSE

To provide attractively served food to the patient in an efficient manner.

PROCEDURE

1. Check list of patients who are not permitted food or fluids by mouth.
2. Clear bedside or overbed table.
3. Place table within reach of patient.
4. Place patient in comfortable position.
5. Wash hands. Wheel cart with trays to unit.
6. Take tray from cart and check to see if it is complete.
7. Read tray card.
8. See that tray is served to patient listed on the selective menus or the Special Diet Request that is placed on each tray.
9. Call each patient by name or check his identification band. Place his tray within easy reach.
10. Feed patient or assist him as necessary such as buttering his bread, cutting his meat, etc. Allow patient to do as much for himself as possible.
11. Make rounds to check that each patient entitled to a tray has been fed. The Diet List may be used as a check off list.
12. After the patient has finished eating, collect tray immediately and return to cart. Make a note of food eaten and record on Intake and Output Sheet as indicated.
13. Report all complaints about food to Food Service.

POINTS TO EMPHASIZE

1. Serve trays promptly.
2. Do not hurry patient.
3. Make rounds to check that all patients have been fed.

10. CARE OF ICE MACHINE AND HANDLING OF ICE, BEDSIDE PITCHERS, AND GLASSES

PURPOSE

To prevent ice machines from becoming a source of infection due to cross-contamination.

EQUIPMENT

To clean and disinfect ice machine:
- Clean gloves, disposable
- 4x4 sponges
- Scouring powder
- Sodium hypochlorite
- Clean 1 gallon container
- Clean ice scoop

PROCEDURE

1. Disconnect ice machine from electrical outlet.
2. Wash hands.
3. Use ice scoop to dispose of any existing ice. Pour tap water into ice storage compartment to melt any remaining ice.
4. Put on gloves and remove scale and other debris with 4x4 sponges and scouring powder.
5. Rinse thoroughly with tap water.
6. Place 1/2 ounce of sodium hypocholrite in 1 gallon of water.
7. Using 4 x 4's wipe all accessible areas of interior with sodium hypochlorite solution. Pay particualr attention to ice chute.
8. Repeat step #7.
9. Allow solution to remain in machine for 30 minutes.
10. Rinse thoroughly with clean tap water three times.
11. Clean the exterior of the ice machine.
12. Connect ice machine to electrical outlet.

POINTS TO EMPHASIZE

1. Keep exterior of machine clean between weekly disinfecting of interior.
2. Limit access to ice machine to nursing service personnel.
3. Always keep door closed when not removing ice.
4. Locate ice machine in a "clean" area of the ward or hospital.
5. If ice must be transported, containers should be clean and covered.
6. Use a scoop or tongs when handling ice. Never handle ice with bare hands.
7. Never store the scoop in the ice when not in use.

CARE OF ICE MACHINE AND HANDLING OF
ICE, BEDSIDE PITCHERS, AND GLASSES (Continued)

POINTS TO EMPHASIZE (Continued)

8. The scoop or tongs must be sanitized at least daily.
9. Each patient should have his own bedside water pitcher with cover.
10. Glasses used for drinking water should be sent to the kitchen for exchange of clean glasses on a routine basis.
11. Culture ice machines according to local hospital policy and record in ice culture log.

CARE OF EQUIPMENT

1. Discard disposable equipment.
2. Replace cleaning gear.

11. FEEDING THE HELPLESS PATIENT

PURPOSE

To promote adequate nutrition of the helpless patient.
To encourage self-help when condition permits.

PROCEDURE

1. Place the patient in a sitting position unless otherwise ordered.
2. Place a towel across the patient's chest. Tuck a napkin under his chin.
3. Place tray on overbed table or bedside stand.
4. Give the patient a piece of buttered bread if he is able to hold it.
5. Feed the patient in the order in which he likes to be fed.
6. Offer liquids during the meal. Have patient use a drinking tube if necessary.
7. Give a small amount of food at one time. Allow the patient to chew and swallow food before offering him more. Do not rush your patient.
8. If patient is inclined to talk, talk with him.
9. Note amount of food he has taken. Record amount of fluid if on measured intake and output.
10. Remove tray. Leave patient comfortable.

POINTS TO EMPHASIZE

1. As you are feeding a blind patient tell him what you are offering and whether it is hot or cold.
2. Encourage a blind patient to begin feeding himself as soon as he is able and when indicated.
3. When encouraging a blind patient to feed himself, arrange tray the same way each time. Place foods on plate in the same clockwise direction and fill glasses and cups one-half full to avoid spilling.
4. If patient has difficulty in swallowing, have oral suction machine at bedside.

12. EVENING CARE

PURPOSE

To relax and prepare patient for the night.
To observe the patient's condition.

EQUIPMENT

Basin of warm water
Towel, washcloth and soap
Toothbrush, and dentifrice/mouthwash
Curved basin
Glass of water
Rubbing alcohol/skin lotion
Comb

PROCEDURE

1. Offer bedpan and urinal.
2. Give oral hygiene.
3. Wash patient's face and hands.
4. Wash back. Give back rub. Comb hair.
5. Straighten and tighten bottom sheets.
6. Freshen pillows.
7. Place extra blanket at foot of bed if weather is cool.
8. Make provision for ventilation of unit.
9. Clean and straighten unit and remove excess gear.

POINTS TO EMPHASIZE

1. Indicated for all bed patients and those on limited activity.
2. Change soiled linen as necessary.
3. Patient may assist with care as condition permits.
4. Ask the patient if soap may be used on the face.
5. Screen patients who require the use of bedpan.

13. CARE OF THE SERIOUSLY ILL PATIENT

PURPOSE

To provide optimum care and close observation of the seriously ill patient.
To keep the patient mentally and physically comfortable.

EQUIPMENT

Special mouth care tray
Rubbing alcohol/skin lotion
Bed linen as necessary
Pillow and/or supporting appliances
Special equipment as needed:

- I.V. Standard
- Suction machine
- Oxygen
- Drainage bottles
- Intake and Output work sheet

PROCEDURE

1. Place patient where he can be easily and <u>closely</u> observed.
2. Keep room quiet, clean and clear of excess gear.
3. Bathe patient daily and P.R.N.
4. Maintain good oral hygiene every 2-4 hours.
5. Wash, rub back and change position every 2 hours unless contraindicated.
6. Speak to patient in a calm, natural tone of voice even if he appears to be unconscious.
7. Report any sudden change in condition.
8. Keep an accurate intake and output record if ordered.
9. Offer fluids if patient is conscious and is able to take them.
10. Record and Report:
    a. Changes in T.P.R. and blood pressure.
    b. State of consciousness.
    c. All observations.

CARE OF THE SERIOUSLY ILL PATIENT (Continued)

POINTS TO EMPHASIZE

1. All patients are seen by a chaplain when they are placed on the Serious or Very Seriously ill list.
2. Be considerate and kind to the patient's relatives.
3. Keep charting up-to-date.
4. Do not discuss patient's condition when the conversation might be overheard by the patient or unauthorized persons.
5. Refer all questions concerning the patient's condition to the doctor or nurse.
6. Be sure all procedures for placing a patient on the SL or VSL have been completed; for exmaple, inventory of personal effects and valuables.

BASIC NURSING PROCEDURES: TAKING TEMPERATURE, PULSE, AND BLOOD PRESSURE

CONTENTS

		Page
I.	TAKING ORAL TEMPERATURE	
	A. Thermometers Disinfected on Ward	1
	B. Individual Thermometer Technique	4
	C. Taking Temperatures With the Electronic Thermometer	6
II.	TAKING AXILLARY TEMPERATURE	7
III.	TAKING RECTAL TEMPERATURE	8
	A. Thermometers Disinfected on Ward	8
	B. Thermometers Disinfected in Central Supply Room	9
IV.	TAKING PULSE AND RESPIRATION	10
V.	APICAL-RADIAL PULSE	11
VI.	TAKING BLOOD PRESSURE	12
VII.	RECORDING ON THE TEMPERATURE, PULSE, AND RESPIRATION FORM	13
VIII.	RECORDING ON PLOTTING CHART	19

BASIC NURSING PROCEDURES: TAKING TEMPERATURE, PULSE, AND BLOOD PRESSURE

I. TAKING ORAL TEMPERATURE
A. THERMOMETERS DISINFECTED ON WARD

PURPOSE

To determine the patient's body temperature as recorded on a clinical thermometer.

EQUIPMENT

1. Tray containing:
    a. Two containers of disinfecting agent marked #1 and #2
    b. Container of green soap solution
    c. Container of water
    d. Container of clean cotton
    e. Waste container for soiled cotton
    f. Minimum of 6 thermometers, 3 in each container of disinfecting solution
    g. T.P.R. book
    h. Pencil and pen
    i. Watch with second hand

PROCEDURE

1. Take equipment to bedside.
2. Tell the patient what you are going to do.
3. Remove thermometer from container #1.
4. Wipe thermometer (over waste container) with water moistened sponge from stem to bulb using rotary motion. Discard sponge in waste container.
5. Shake down thermometer mercury to 95° F.
6. Place thermometer under patient's tongue. Caution him to keep his lips closed.
7. Distribute other thermometers to second and third patients in same manner.
8. Take third patient's pulse and respiration. Record results in T.P.R. book.
9. Take pulse and respiration of second patient, record, then first patient. Record results in T.P.R. book.
10. Remove thermometer from first patient's mouth after 3 minutes.
11. Wash thermometer (over waste container) with soap-moistened sponge from stem to bulb using rotary motion. Discard sponge in waste container.

PROCEDURE (Continued)

12. Moisten cotton sponge with water and wipe thermometer from stem to bulb in a rotary container. Discard sponge in waste container.
13. Read thermometer. Record results in T.P.R. book.
14. Place thermometer in the <u>original</u> container of disinfecting agent.
15. Repeat the steps 10 through 13 for second and third patients.
16. Disinfect these thermometers for a minimum of 20 minutes (depending on disinfecting agent used).
17. Continue using thermometers from alternate containers until all patient's temperatures have been taken.
18. Record T.P.R.'s on SP 511.

CARE OF EQUIPMENT

1. After each use
   a. Remove waste.
   b. Clean tray.
   c. Reset tray.
   d. Replace solutions (water - soap).
2. Daily
   a. Wash containers in warm, soapy water, rinse and dry.
   b. Change all solutions.
   c. Wash thermometers in cold, soapy water, rinse and place in disinfecting agent.
   d. Refill and reset tray.

POINTS TO EMPHASIZE

1. Wait for 10 minutes before taking temperature of patient who has had hot or cold drink or who has been smoking.
2. Be sure thermometer reads 95 or below before using it.
3. Encircle abnormal vital signs with red pencil in T.P.R. book.
4. Report all abnormal vital signs to Charge Nurse.
5. Describe quality of pulse and respiration in the observation column on Nursing Notes (SF 510).

POINTS TO EMPHASIZE (Continued)

6. After washing thermometer with soap, be sure to rinse well with water before putting it into disinfectant, as bacterial action is nullified in the presence of soap; for example, Zephiran chloride and iodine preparations.
7. Individual thermometers should be used for patients suspected of having a communicable disease.

THERMOMETERS STERILIZED IN CENTRAL SUPPLY ROOM

EQUIPMENT

1. Tray containing:
   a. Container of sterile oral thermometers that are sealed in paper envelopes.
   b. Container of green soap solution.
   c. Container of clean cotton.
   d. Container for waste material.
   e. T.P.R. book.
   f. Pencil.
   g. Watch with second hand.

PROCEDURE

1. Tell the patient what you are going to do.
2. Remove thermometer from envelope.
3. Shake thermometer mercury to 95° F.
4. Place thermometer under patient's tongue. Caution him to keep his lips closed.
5. Take, record and report vital signs as in previous procedure, numbers 7 through 11, pages 25 and 26.

CARE OF EQUIPMENT

1. After each use:
   a. Empty container of waste cotton.
   b. Return container of soiled thermometers to CSR in accordance with local instructions and exchange for an adequate supply of clean thermometers.
   c. Reset tray.
2. Daily:
   a. Wash containers in warm, soapy water, rinse and dry.
   b. Refill and reset tray.

TAKING ORAL TEMPERATURE
B. INDIVIDUAL THERMOMETER TECHNIQUE

PURPOSE

To determine the patient's body temperature as recorded on a clinical thermometer.

EQUIPMENT

1. Individual thermometer for each patient at bedside
2. Plastic thermometer holder with disinfectant solution - protective container of 2 1/2 cc. disposable syringe can be used
3. Adhesive tape
4. Container of clean cotton balls
5. Container for soiled cotton balls
6. T.P.R. book and pen
7. Watch with second hand

PROCEDURE

1. Upon admission, set up thermometer and holder at patient's unit:
    a. Fill thermometer holder (protective container from a 2 1/2 cc. disposable syringe) with disinfectant.
    b. Place thermometer inside container.
    c. Tape container to head of bed or side of bedside locker.
2. When taking temperatures:
    a. Take containers for cotton balls to bedside.
    b. Tell patient what you are going to do.
    c. Remove thermometer from holder.
    d. Wipe thermometer with clean cotton ball. Discard cotton ball in waste container.
    e. Shake down thermometer mercury to $95°$ F.
    f. Place thermometer under patient's tongue.
    g. Follow above steps to second and third patient,
    h. Take third patient's pulse and respiration. Record results in T.P.R. book.
    i. Take pulse and respiration of second patient, record, then first patient,
    j. Remove thermometer from first patient's mouth after 3 minutes.
    k. Wipe thermometer with clean cotton ball. Discard cotton ball in waste container.
    l. Read thermometer and replace in holder. Record results in T.P.R. book,
    m. Repeat steps j through l for second and third patient.

CARE OF EQUIPMENT
1. After each use:
   a. Discard soiled cotton balls and container.
2. Weekly and when patient is discharged:
   a. Collect thermometers and holders.
   b. Disinfect thermometers as outlined on page 26.
   c. Place in new holders containing disinfectant.
   d. Discard old holders.
   e. Replace thermometers and holders at bedside.

C. TAKING TEMPERATURES WITH THE ELECTRONIC THERMOMETER

PURPOSE
To determine the patient's body temperature with an electronic thermometer which is a beat sending device with an accuracy of a plus or minus of .2 degrees. It utilizes a disposable probe cover and records oral and rectal temperatures within 15 seconds.

EQUIPMENT
1. Base for electronic thermometer
2. Thermometer with oral probe (sensing device)
3. Rectal probes where applicable
4. Disposable probe covers

PROCEDURE
1. Remove probe from base which is connected to electricity.
2. Attach strap of thermometer around shoulder to secure thermometer to side (left side if right handed).
3. Remove probe and insert probe into disposable probe cover.
4. Turn thermometer on by pressing small bar on top.
5. Place covered probe into patient's mouth in the sublingual area and slowly push probe along the base of the tongue as far back as possible without discomfort to the patient.
6. Hold probe in place until indicator on thermometer records a completed thermometer reading.
7. Transfer reading to appropriate records.
8. Eject the disposable probe cover.
9. Press bar on back of thermometer erasing present reading and repeat the above procedure for the next patient.
10. Remove thermometer pack and replace securely in base for recharging thermometer.

POINTS TO EMPHASIZE
1. Grasp probe at reinforced area in the center to decrease breakage.
2. Always keep base plugged into electrical current.
3. Always keep thermometer in base when not in use to keep the battery charged.
4. Use specified probe for rectal temperature and insert probe cover 1/2 inch on adults or 1/4 inch on babies for accurate recordings.
5. For axillary temperatures do not press bar to activate thermometer until the oral probe with cover is in place, then allow 60-90 seconds for recording of temperature. Indicator will not come on.

II. TAKING AXILLARY TEMPERATURE

PURPOSE

To determine a patient's temperature when the oral or rectal route is contraindicated.

EQUIPMENT

Oral thermometer tray
T.P.R. book
Pencil or pen
Watch with a second hand

PROCEDURE

Same as for oral temperature (pages 1 and 2) except:
1. Wipe axilla dry.
2. Place oral thermometer in axilla. Have patient cross arms over chest.
3. Leave thermometer in place for 10 minutes.
4. Write "A" above temperature in T.P.R. book, and T.P.R. graph (SF 511).

III. TAKING RECTAL TEMPERATURE
A. THERMOMETERS DISINFECTED ON WARD

PURPOSE
To determine patient's temperature when the oral method is contraindicated.

EQUIPMENT
1. Tray containing
   a. Two containers of disinfecting agent marked #1 and #2
   b. Container of green soap solution
   c. Container of water
   d. Container of clean cotton sponges
   e. Container for waste cotton sponges
   f. Minimum of 4 thermometers in container #1 of disinfecting agent. (Number of thermometers determined by ward needs).
   g. Tube of water soluble lubricant
   h. T.P.R. book
   i. Pencil and pen
   j. Watch with second hand

PROCEDURE
1. Take equipment to bedside.
2. Tell patient what you are going to do.
3. Remove thermometer from container fl.
4. Wipe thermometer (over waste container) with water moistened sponge from stem to bulb using a rotary motion. Discard sponge in waste container.
5. Shake thermometer mercury to 95° F.
6. Lubricate thermometer with water soluble lubricant.
7. Turn patient on side unless contraindicated.
8. Separate buttocks and gently insert thermometer 1 1/2 inches into the rectum in an upward and forward direction. Insert 1/2 - 3/4 inch in infants and children.
9. Hold thermometer in place for 5 minutes. Count pulse and respiration and record in T.P.R. book.
10. Remove thermometer.
11. Wash thermometer (over waste container) with soap moistened sponge from stem to bulb using rotary motion. Discard sponge in waste container.
12. Moisten cotton sponge with water and wipe thermometer from stem to bulb in a rotary motion. Discard sponge in waste container.
13. Read thermometer and record temperature in T.P.R. book. Place "R" above recording to indicate that it was taken rectally.
14. Return thermometer to glass #2 for sterilization for a minimum of 20 minutes.
15. Leave patient in comfortable position.

16. Record T.P.R.'s on SF 511. Use "R" to indicate rectal temperature.
17. Continue taking additional rectal temperatures in the same manner.

CARE OF EQUIPMENT
1. After each use
   a. Remove waste.
   b. Clean tray.
   c. Transfer thermometers from container 12 to container #1 after 20 minutes has elapsed.
   d. Replace water and soap solution.
   e. Reset tray.
2. Daily
   a. Wash containers in warm, soapy water, rinse and dry.
   b. Change all solutions.
   c. Wash thermometers in cold, soapy water, rinse well and place in disinfectant agent.
   d. Refill and reset tray.

POINTS TO EMPHASIZE
1. Wait 30 minutes before taking temperature on patient who has had an enema.
2. Use only a stub bulb thermometer expressly made for rectal use.
3. Do not leave patient unattended while thermometer is inserted.
4. Report abnormal vital signs to Charge Nurse.
5. Describe the quality of pulse and respirations in observation column on Nursing Notes (SF 510). On wards where many rectal temperatures are taken, (for example, Pediatrics, ICU, etc.), increase the number of thermometers in each container. Continue using thermometers from alternate containers, allowing at least 20 minutes for sterilization, until all patients' temperatures are taken.
6. Be sure to rinse thermometer well before putting it into the disinfectant, as bacterial action is nullified in the presence of soap - for example, Zephiran chloride and iodine preparations.

B. THERMOMETERS DISINFECTED IN CENTRAL SUPPLY ROOM

EQUIPMENT
1. Tray containing
   a. Container of rectal thermometers sealed in paper envelopes
   b. Container of clean cotton sponges
   c. Container of soap solution
   d. Container for waste cotton sponges
   e. Container for used thermometers
   f. Tube of water soluble lubricant

g. T.P.R. book
h. Pencil or pen
i. Watch with second hand

PROCEDURE
1. Remove thermometer from envelope.
2. Take, record and report vital signs as in previous procedure page 30.
3. Return thermometer to container of soap solution for return to C.S.R.

CARE OF EQUIPMENT
1. After each use
   Remove waste
   Clean tray
2. Daily
   Return container of thermometers to C.S.R. in accordance with local instructions and exchange for supply of sterile thermometers.
   Wash containers in warm/ soapy water, rinse and dry.
   Refill and reset tray.

IV. TAKING PULSE AND RESPIRATION

PURPOSE

To determine the character and rate of the pulse and respiration.

EQUIPMENT
Watch with a second hand
Pencil or pen
T. P. R. book

PROCEDURE
1. Tell patient what he is to do.
2. Have the patient lie down or sit in chair. Draw his arm and hand across his chest.
3. Place three fingers over the radial artery on the thumb side of the patient's wrist. Use just enough pressure to feel the pulse beat.
4. Observe the general character of the pulse, then count the number of beats for 30 seconds, multiply by two. If any deviation from normal or irregularity is noted, count for one full minute.
5. With the fingers still on the wrist, count the rise and fall of the chest or upper abdomen for 30 seconds, multiply by 2. If any irregularity or difficulty is noted, count for one full minute.
5. Record in T. P. R. book and report any abnormality.

POINTS TO EMPHASIZE
DO NOT use thumb when taking pulse beat.

V. APICAL-RADIAL PULSE

PURPOSE
To compare the pulse rate of the heart at the apex and the pulse rate in the radial artery.

EQUIPMENT
Stethoscope
Watch with second hand

PROCEDURE
1. Tell patient what you are going to do.
2. Have patient lie quietly in bed.
3. Open pajama coat to expose chest.
4. One person standing on the left side of the bed places a stethoscope over apex of heart (slightly below and to the right of the left nipple) to locate the apical heart beat.
5. Another person standing on the right side of bed locates the radial pulse; hold watch so that it can be seen by both people.
6. Using the same watch and at a signal from the person taking the apical pulse, both people count for one minute.
7. Replace pajama coat; leave patient comfortable.
8. Record in observation column on Nursing Notes (SF 510). Example: Apical 92. Radial 86.

POINTS TO EMPHASIZE
Two corpsmen are necessary to carry out this procedure because the two pulses must be taken at the same time to compare rates.

CARE OF EQUIPMENT
1. Wipe earpieces and diaphragm/bell of stethoscope with alcohol sponges before and after procedure.
2. Return stethoscope to proper place.

VI. TAKING BLOOD PRESSURE

PURPOSE
To determine the pressure which the blood exerts against the walls of the vessels.

EQUIPMENT
Sphygmomanometer
Stethoscope
Pencil and paper
Alcohol sponges

PROCEDURE
1. Tell patient what you are going to do.
2. Place patient in comfortable position sitting or lying down.
3. Place rubber portion of cuff over the brachial artery. Secure either by hooking or wrapping depending on the type of apparatus.
4. Clip indicator to cuff (aneroid) or place apparatus on a level surface (mercury) at about heart level. Make sure the tubing is not kinked and that it does not rub against the apparatus.
5. Locate brachial pulse at bend of elbow.
6. Place stethoscope in ears with ear pieces pointing forward.
7. Hold stethoscope in place over the brachial artery. Inflate cuff until the indicator registers 200 mm. Loosen thumb screw of valve and allow air to escape slowly.
8. Listen for the sounds. Watch the indicator. Note where the first distinct rhythmic sound is heard. This is the Systolic Pressure.
9. Continue releasing air from the cuff. Note where sound changes to dull muffled beat. This is the Diastolic Pressure.
10. Open valve completely. Release all air from cuff.
11. Remove cuff. Record reading.

POINTS TO EMPHASIZE
1. Either arm may be used in taking blood pressure, but in repeating readings, it is important to use the same arm.
2. Some departments in the hospital may define diastolic pressure as the last sound heard.
3. If unsure of reading, completely deflate cuff and repeat procedure.

CARE OF EQUIPMENT
1. Fold and replace cuff.
2. Wipe ear pieces and bell/diaphragm of stethoscope with alcohol sponge before and after procedure. Replace.

VII. RECORDING ON THE TEMPERATURE, PULSE, AND RESPIRATION FORM

PURPOSE

To keep an accurate and up-to-date record of the patient's cardinal or vital signs.

EQUIPMENT

Pen with black or blue-black ink
Standard Form 511, Temperature-Pulse-Respiration
Ruler
Addressograph plate

PROCEDURE

1. Complete identifying data in lower left corner of SF-511.
2. Fill in spaces as indicated in the heading by printing:
   Month
   Date of month.
   Hospital day.
   Postoperative or postpartum day.
   Hours T.P.R's are taken.
3. Using a small dot, record temperature and pulse in spaces corresponding vertically to hour and horizontally to scales on left side of form. Join dots of previous readings by drawing straight lines with ruler.
4. Print respiration rate in space indicated to correspond with date and hour taken.
5. Record blood pressure in space indicated to correspond with date and hour taken.
6. Record height and weight on admission in spaces provided. Repeated weight recordings are made to correspond with date and hour taken.

POINTS TO EMPHASIZE

1. For every four hour and twice a day temperature and pulse, record within dotted lines.
2. For four times a day temperature and pulse, record on dotted lines.
3. Blood pressures required more than twice a day should be graphed on a Plotting Chart (SF 512).
4. Any pecularities of the patient that affects the temperature, pulse, or respiration, i.e.; drop in temperature due to medication; ongoing cooling procedure; and/or absences from ward, may be recorded in ..graphic column at the designated time.
5. Indicate method - if axillary or rectal is used.

SAMPLE TEMPERATURE - PULSE - RESPIRATION (SF511)

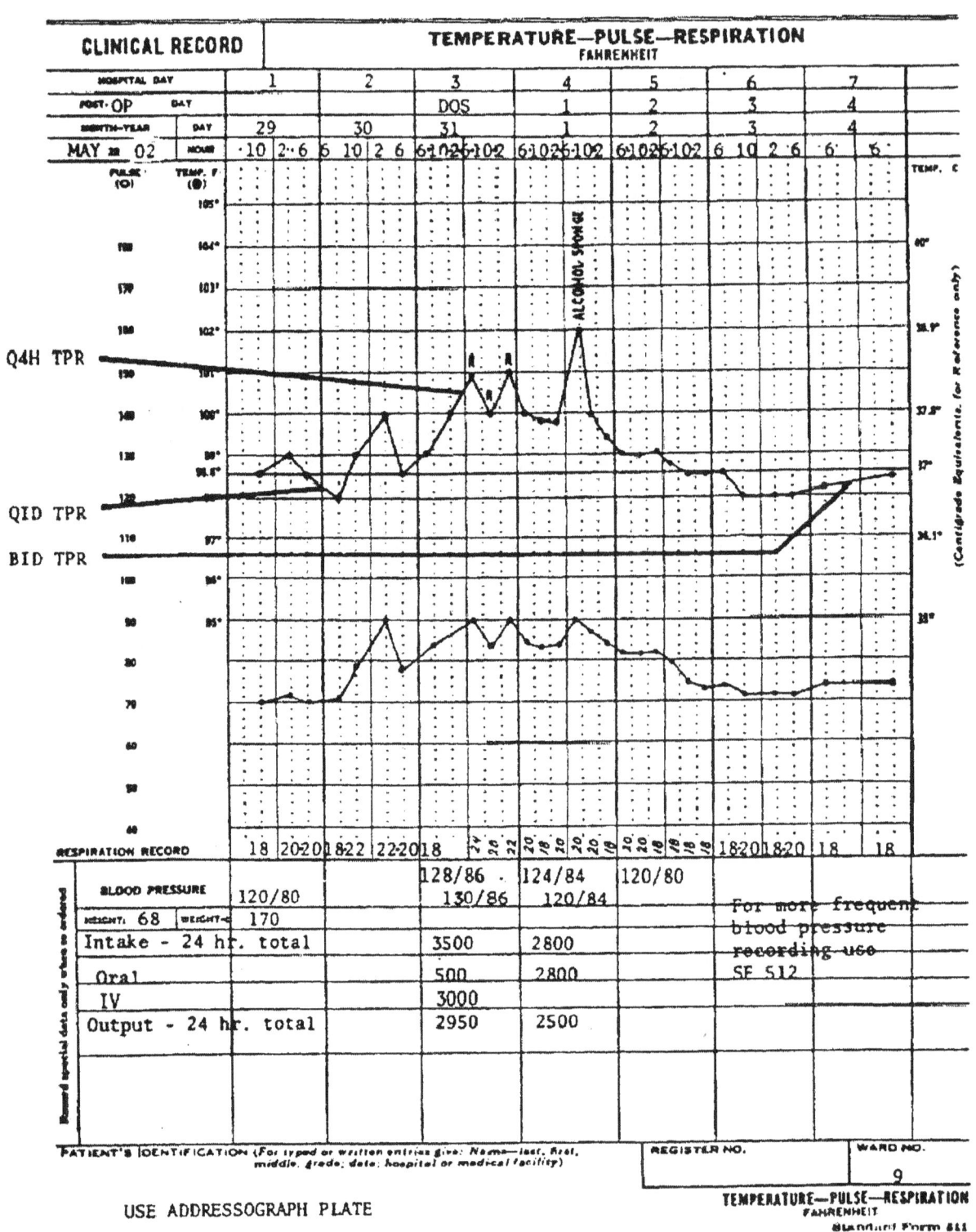

USING THE TEMPERATURE - PULSE - RESPIRATION GRAPHIC FORM 511

All entries shall be lettered in black or blue-black ink. Ballpoint pens may be used. Each sheet should have identifying data at the foot of each page. These data should be legible, correct and complete.

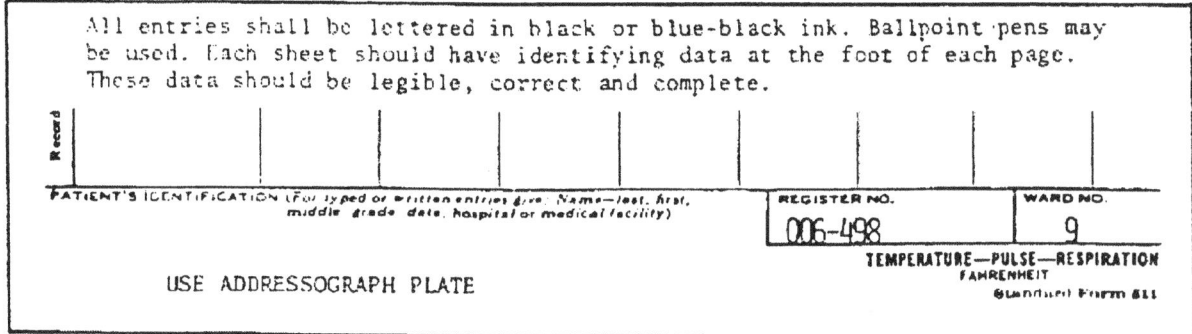

Each sheet is divided into seven major columns, one for each day of the week. The day of admission is the first hospital day.

The month, day of the month, and year appear in the spaces for that purpose. In the sample below, the patient was admitted to the hospital on May 7, 2002.

The day of operation or delivery is lettered "Operation" or "Delivery". The following day is the first postoperative or postdelivery day. For example, if the patient had surgery on his third hospital day, the chart would appear as follows:

To chart the temperature and pulse, place a dot on the graph according to the scale on the left in the vertical column that designates the correct time and date. Connect the dot of the previous recording with a solid line.

The respirations are recorded in the vertical column according to the hour.

In the sample at the left the 6 a.m. TPR was 97-72-16. The 6 p.m. TPR was 98.6-76-18.

Each day is divided into two columns, a.m. and p.m.

The a.m. and p.m. subdivision is further divided by two vertical dotted lines. For every four hour temperature and pulse reading, place the recordings WITHIN the dotted lines.

- 2 a.m.
- 6 a.m.
- 10 a.m.
- 2 p.m.
- 6 p.m.
- 10 p.m.

Twice a day temperature and pulse recordings are placed WITHIN the dotted lines in the center of the a.m. and p.m. column.

- 6 a.m.
- 6 p.m.

For four-times-a-day readings, place the recordings ON the dotted lines.

- 6 a.m.
- 10 a.m.
- 2 p.m.
- 6 p.m.

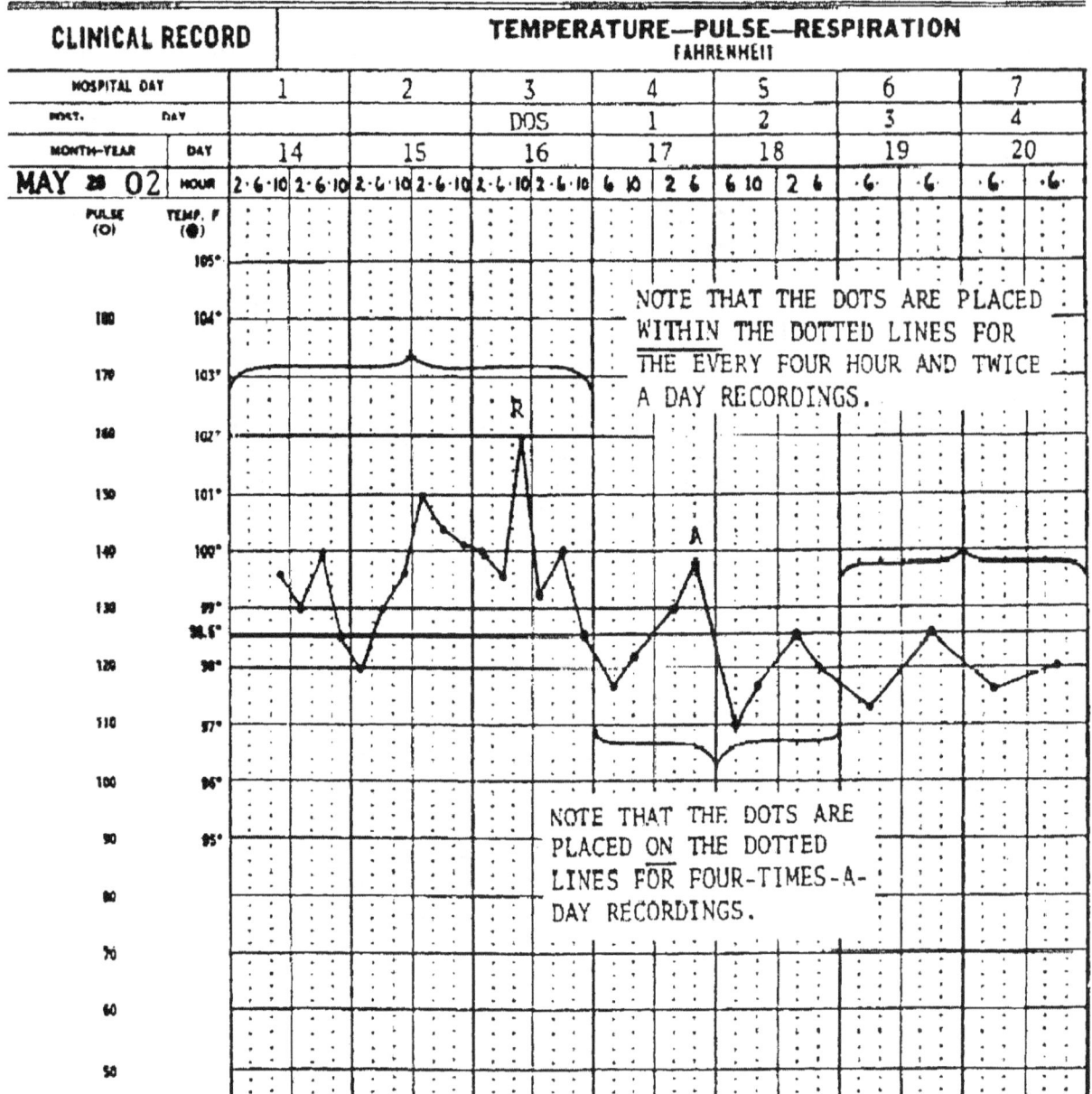

If a temperature is taken by rectum, place an "R" (for rectal) above the dot on the graph.
If a temperature is taken by axilla, place an "A" (for axillary) above the dot on the graph.

VIII. RECORDING ON PLOTTING CHART

PURPOSE

To keep an accurate, visible record of repeated observations of intake-output, weight, blood pressure, etc.

EQUIPMENT

Pen with, black or blue-black ink
Standard Form 512, Plotting Chart
Ruler

PROCEDURE

1. Complete identifying data in lower left corner of chart. (Page 25)
2. Print date and purpose in upper left corner.
3. Calibrate measurements along vertical portion of graph:
    Start scale at bottom working toward top at a definite and uniform rate of progression, as 0-10-20.30.
    Label scale at top to show unit of measure as cc. , lbs. , or mm.
4. Note date time intervals of measure along top horizontal portion of graph.
5. Show meaning of symbols used in a key to the side of graph.

Note: Red pencil may be ued when filling in bar graphs.

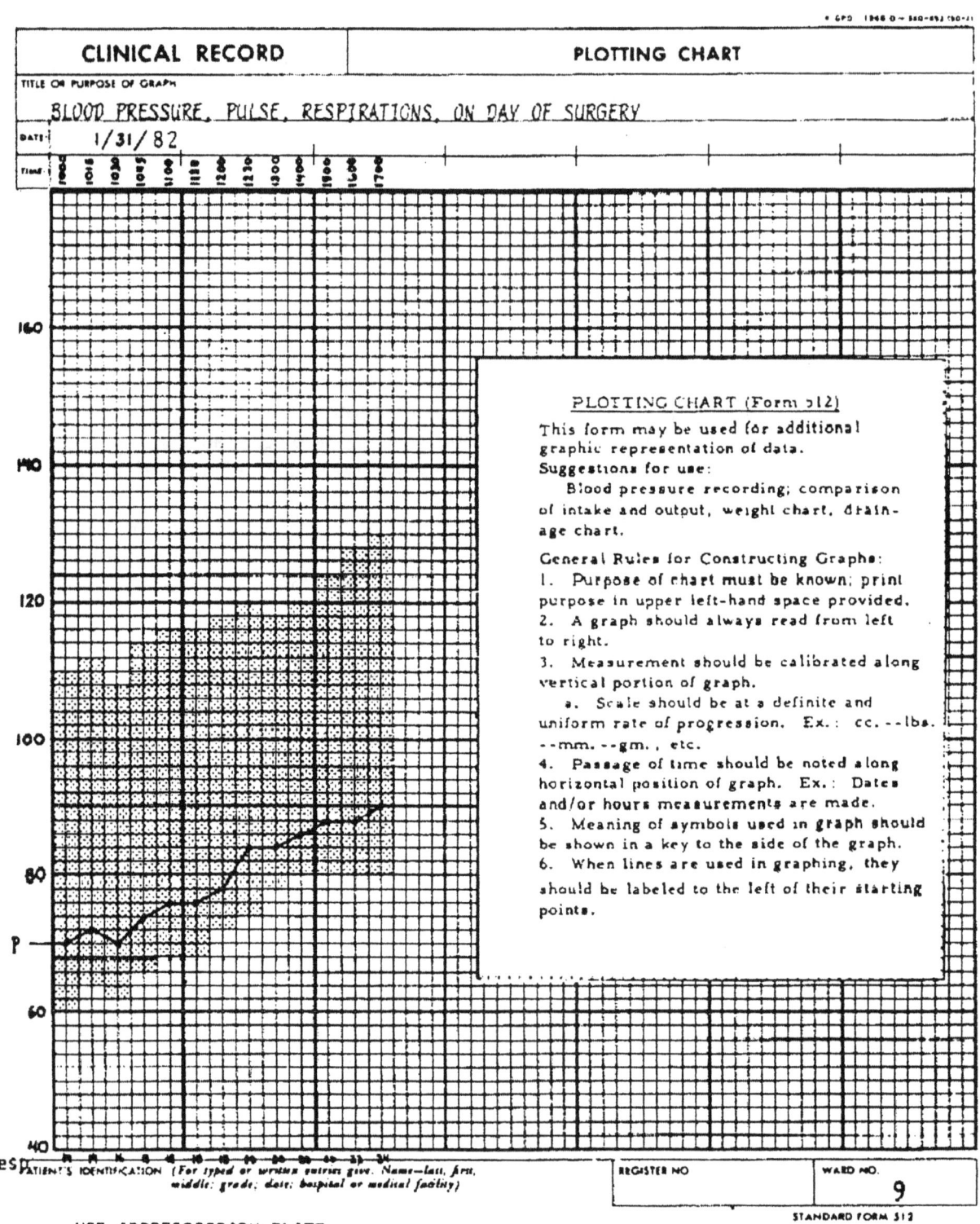

BASIC FUNDAMENTALS OF MEDICATION ADMINISTRATION

CONTENTS

	Page
I. GUIDELINES FOR MEDICATION ADMINISTRATION	1
A. General	1
B. Unit Dose	3
II. MEDICATION ADMINISTRATION RECORD	4
III. DROPS	7
A. Ear	7
B. Eye	8
C. Nose	9
IV. GASTRIC TUBES	10
V. HEPARIN LOCKS	11
VI. INJECTIONS	12
A. General	12
B. Intramuscular	14
1. Z-Tract	15
C. Intradermal	15
D. Intravenous Piggyback	16
E. Subcutaneous	18
1. Insulin	18
VII. ORAL MEDICATIONS	19
A. Tablets, Pills, or Capsules	20
B. Powders	20
C. Liquids	20
VIII. SUPPOSITORIES	21
A. Rectal	21
B. Urethral	22
C. Vaginal	23

BASIC FUNDAMENTALS OF MEDICATION ADMINISTRATION

I. GUIDELINES FOR MEDICATION ADMINISTRATION

A. General

PURPOSE

To administer the right medication, in the right dose, by the right route, to the right patient, at the right time

PROCEDURE	SPECIAL CONSIDERATIONS

• Transcribe medication and treatment orders from doctor's orders to
  • Medication and Treatment Cards
  • Nursing Care Plan
  • Medication Administration Record (MAR)
	Follow local policy.

• Check ALL Medication and Treatment Cards against Nursing Care Plan at the beginning of each shift.	
• Return cards to medication and treatment board, placing each card in space corresponding to hour when medication is due. • Clean working area.	
• Wash your hands.	
• Obtain supplies and equipment such as tongue blades, paper cups, pitcher of water, medication tray or cart, and stethoscope.	Keep cards for same patient together.

• Separate cards into
  • oral medications
  • injections
  • treatments	

• Arrange cards in sequence similar to placement of patients on ward.	
•Turn cards face down, turn top card up, and read information on card.	
• Locate medication and compare label on medication with name of medication and dosage on card.	FIRST MEDICATION CHECK.

GUIDELINES FOR MEDICATION ADMINISTRATION, GENERAL (cont)

PROCEDURE	SPECIAL CONSIDERATIONS
• Remove medication container and compare label on container with name of medication and dosage on card.	SECOND CHECK.
• Pour required dosage and compare label on container with card for name of medication and dosage.	THIRD CHECK.
• Place medication and card on tray or cart.	NEVER leave medication cart or tray unattended.
• Continue with remaining cards in same manner.	
• Lock medication cabinet before leaving the area.	
• Administer only medications that you personally prepared.	NEVER allow others to administer medication that you prepared.
• Check name on bed tag with name on card.	FIRST ID CHECK.
• Compare name on card with patient's ID band.	SECOND CHECK.
• Ask patient: "What is your name?" Be sure response is accurate.	THIRD CHECK.
• Administer medication ONLY if all 3 checks agree.	
• Place card face down on one side of tray.	
• Continue to administer medications until all are given.	
• Reset tray or cart for next use.	
• Take cards to desk.	
• Record medications, time and date given, and your initials on MAR using cards as guide.	
• Replace cards on board at next hour due.	

B. *Unit Dose*

PURPOSE

To administer single-dose medication in ready-to-use form

PROCEDURE	SPECIAL CONSIDERATIONS
• See "Guidelines for Medication Administration, General."	
• Get stocked medication cart from storage area.	Cart is stocked by pharmacy personnel.
• Unlock cart.	
• Wheel medication cart to bedside, check MAR, and identify patient.	Follow local policy.

• Open cassette drawer.
  • Read MAR.
  • Select medication from cassette drawer.	

• Check medication against MAR for date, dosage, and route.	

• Administer medication and record immediately on MAR.
  • Remain with patient until medication has been taken.
  • Replace drawer in correct space in cassette.	

• Dispose of litter, syringe, and needle before moving to next patient.
  • Break off tip of needle and syringe, and dispose in dirty needle box.
  • Place glass unit dose liquid container in bag for return to pharmacy.	

• Lock cart and return to storage area.	

II. MEDICATION ADMINISTRATION RECORD (MAR)

PURPOSE
To maintain a permanent record of medication administered

PROCEDURE	SPECIAL CONSIDERATIONS
•Stamp MAR with Addressograph as shown in figure 6-1 on the following page.	
• Enter ward number at bottom right of form; record month and year in space provided at the top.	Make all entries in black ink.
• Transcribe scheduled medications from doctor's orders to front of form.	
• Enter order date, medication dosage, frequency, and route of administration.	
• Complete "Hours" column to indicate scheduled hours for administration starting with earliest military time after 2400 hours.	
• Complete "Dates Given" blocks at top of form.	
• Enter month and dates for a 7day period, starting with first day medication is given.	
• Cancel vacant spaces with an "X."	
• Draw a heavy line across page under last entry and enter next medication directly below.	Do not skip a space.
• When medication has been given, enter your initials in column corresponding to date and hour of administration.	
• Place an "*" in column if the medication was not given and state reason on Nursing Notes.	
• Place an "L" under date and opposite hour patient is on liberty.	Follow local policy.
• When medication is stopped, bracket remaining spaces for that day; write "STOPPED," enter date and initials.	Applies to scheduled drugs, PRN, and variable dose medications.
• Complete "Initial Code" section.	

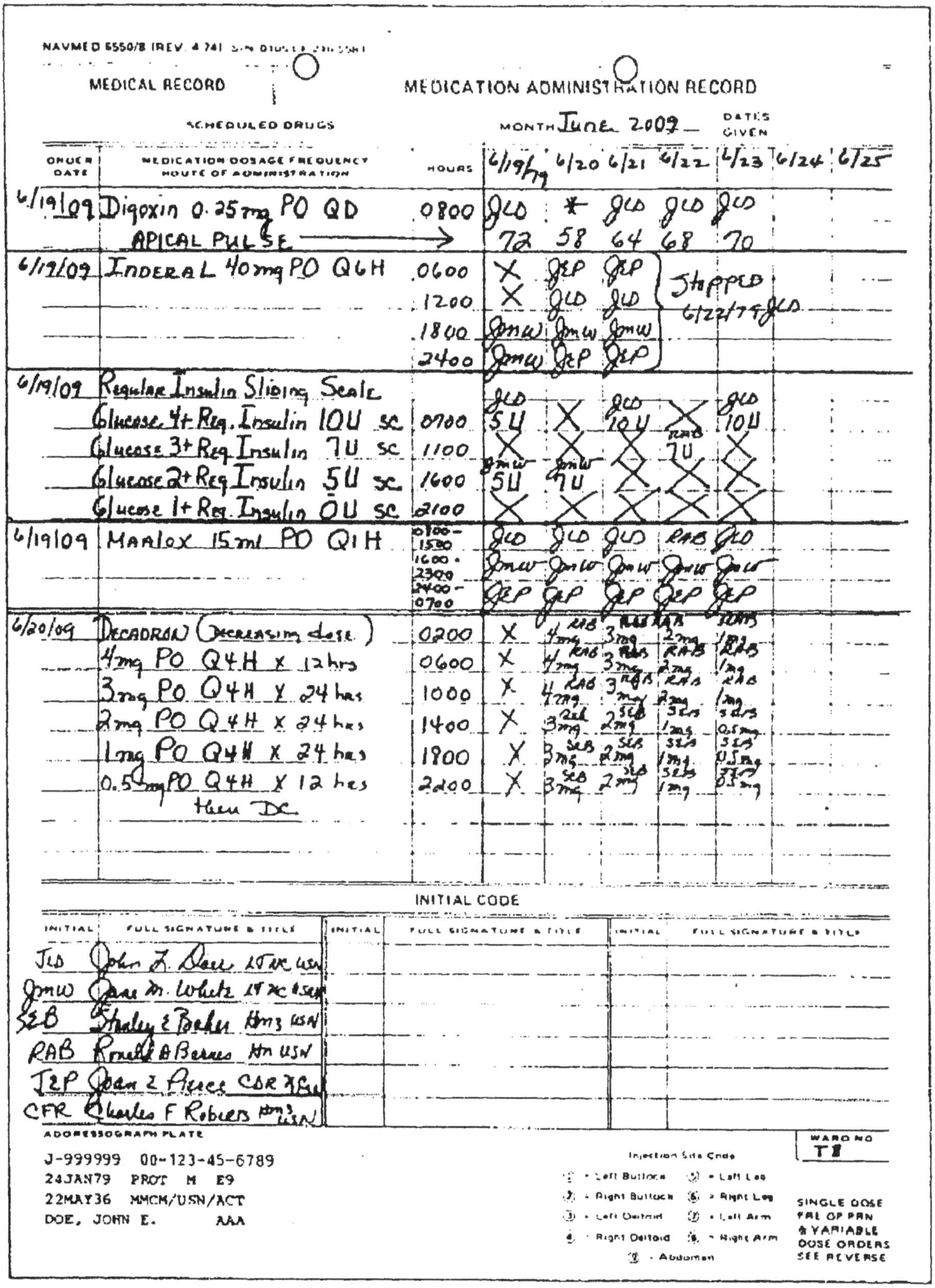

NAVMED 6550/8 (REV. 4-74)

MEDICAL RECORD

MEDICATION ADMINISTRATION RECORD

SCHEDULED DRUGS — MONTH June 2009 — DATES GIVEN

ORDER DATE	MEDICATION-DOSAGE-FREQUENCY ROUTE OF ADMINISTRATION	HOURS	6/19/09	6/20	6/21	6/22	6/23	6/24	6/25
6/19/09	Digoxin 0.25mg PO QD	0800	JLD	*	JLD	JLD	JLD		
	APICAL PULSE →		72	58	64	68	70		
6/19/09	INDERAL 40mg PO Q6H	0600	X	JEP	JEP	Stopped 6/22/09 JLD			
		1200	X	JLD	JLD				
		1800	JMW	JMW	JMW				
		2400	JMW	JEP	JEP				
6/19/09	Regular Insulin Sliding Scale								
	Glucose 4+ Reg. Insulin 10U sc	0700	JLD 5U	X	JLD 10U	X	JLD 10U		
	Glucose 3+ Reg. Insulin 7U sc	1100	X	X	X	RAB 7U	X		
	Glucose 2+ Reg. Insulin 5U sc	1600	JMW 5U	JMW 7U	X	X	X		
	Glucose 1+ Reg. Insulin 0U sc	2100	X	X	X	X	X		
6/19/09	MAALOX 15ml PO Q1H	0700-1500	JLD	JLD	JLD	RAB	JLD		
		1600-2300	JMW	JMW	JMW	JMW	JMW		
		2400-0700	JEP	JEP	JEP	JEP	JEP		
6/20/09	DECADRON (Decreasing dose)	0200	X	4mg RAB	3mg RAB	2mg RAB	1mg SEB		
	4mg PO Q4H x 12hrs	0600	X	4mg RAB	3mg RAB	2mg RAB	1mg RAB		
	3mg PO Q4H x 24hrs	1000	X	4mg RAB	3mg RAB	2mg RAB	1mg RAB		
	2mg PO Q4H x 24hrs	1400	X	3mg SEB	2mg SEB	1mg SEB	0.5mg SEB		
	1mg PO Q4H x 24hrs	1800	X	3mg SEB	2mg SEB	1mg SEB	0.5mg SEB		
	0.5mg PO Q4H x 12hrs then DC	2200	X	3mg SEB	2mg SEB	1mg SEB	0.5mg SEB		

INITIAL CODE

INITIAL	FULL SIGNATURE & TITLE
JLD	John L. Doe LT NC USN
JMW	Jane M. White LT NC USN
SEB	Shirley E Baker HM3 USN
RAB	Ronald A Barnes HN USN
JEP	Joan E Pierce CDR NC USN
CFR	Charles F Roberts HM3 USN

ADDRESSOGRAPH PLATE

J-999999 00-123-45-6789
24JAN79 PROT M E9
22MAY36 MMCM/USN/ACT
DOE, JOHN E. AAA

Injection Site Code: 1 = Left Buttock; 2 = Right Buttock; 3 = Left Deltoid; 4 = Right Deltoid; 5 = Left Leg; 6 = Right Leg; 7 = Left Arm; 8 = Right Arm; 9 = Abdomen

WARD NO T2

SINGLE DOSE PRE OP PRN & VARIABLE DOSE ORDERS SEE REVERSE

Figure 1. Sample Entries on Medication Administration Record (Front).

MEDICATION ADMINISTRATION RECORD (cont)

PROCEDURE

- Transcribe single-order medication, dosage, route of administration, and date and time to be given on back of form. See figure 2 on the following page.

- After administering medication, initial appropriate block.

- Transcribe each preoperative (PREOP) medication dosage, and route of administration on succeeding lines.

- Enter your initials after administering medications.

- Transcribe PRN and variable dose medications from doctor's orders to back of form (fig. 2).

- Enter order date, medication, dosage, frequency, route, and reason for medication.

- Enter date, time, dose, and your initials after administering medication.

NOTE: Some medication orders require modification of basic transcription and charting techniques (fig. 1). These include:

   • increasing or decreasing dose medications
   • medications requiring apical pulse assessment before administration
   • medications administered every other day
   • medications such as insulin administered per sliding scale

SPECIAL CONSIDERATIONS

A bracket may be used to show that all PREOP medications are to be given on the same date and time.

For variable dose medications, the dosage need not be the same for each entry.

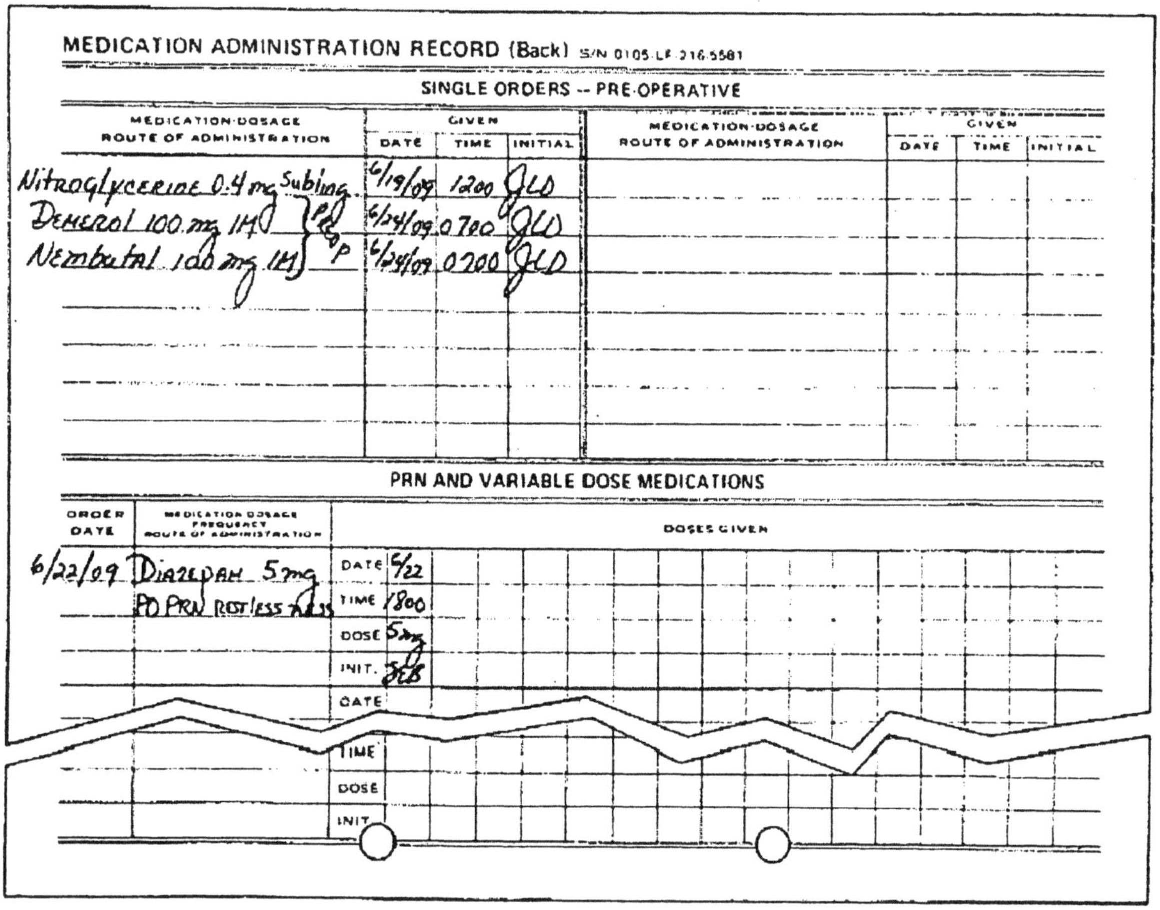

Figure 2. Sample Entries on Medication Administration Record (Back).

III. DROPS
A. Ear

PURPOSE
To instill medication into the auditory canal

PROCEDURE

• See "Guidelines for Medication Administration, General."

• Position patient on side with affected ear upward.

• Clean external auditory canal gently with cotton applicators.

• Straighten auditory canal by gently pulling lobe upward and backward.

SPECIAL CONSIDERATIONS

Patients should have their own properly labeled medication and it should be at room temperature.

Avoid traumatizing when dry-wiping ear canal.

DROPS, EAR (cont)
PROCEDURE

- Instill prescribed number of drops holding dropper nearly horizontally.

- Place cotton loosely in external auditory canal (if ordered).

- Instruct patient to remain in position with treated ear upward for about 5 minutes.

SPECIAL CONSIDERATIONS

Support head as needed. Allow medication to fall to side of canal.

SUPPLIES AND EQUIPMENT

Applicators, cotton tipped   Cotton balls

B. *Eye*
(Ointment Included)

PURPOSE
To apply medication to eye tissue

PROCEDURE

- See "Guidelines for Medication Administration."

- Verify eye to be medicated.

- Tilt patient's head backward and sideways so solution will run away from tear duct.

- Clean eye gently with cotton ball.

- Retract lower lid.

- Instruct patient to look upward.

- Drop medication onto lower lid as shown in figure 3.

SPECIAL CONSIDERATIONS

If both drops and ointment are ordered, instill drops before applying ointment. Patients should have their own properly labeled medication.

Some solutions are toxic if absorbed through the nose or pharynx.

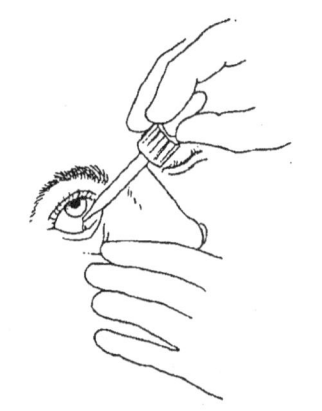

Figure -3. Instilling Eye Drops.

Do not permit dropper or tip of ointment tube to touch the eye. Avoid contaminating medicine container.

DROPS, EYE (cont)
PROCEDURE
• Apply ointment onto conjunctiva of lower lid as illustrated in figure 4.

• Place dropper in bottle or put cap on ointment tube.

• Instruct patient to close eye.

• Wipe excess medication from inner to outer eye with sterile 2x2s then discard.

SPECIAL CONSIDERATIONS

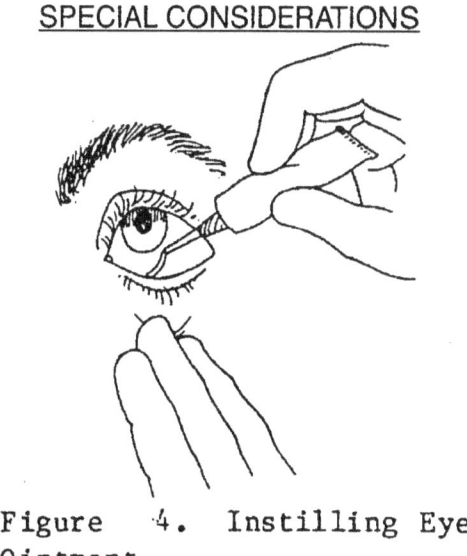

Figure 4. Instilling Eye Ointment.

SUPPLIES AND EQUIPMENT
Cotton balls   Sterile gauze 2x2s

c. *Nose*

PURPOSE
• To instill medication into the nose

PROCEDURE
• See "Guidelines for Medication Administration."

• Tilt patient's head backwards.

• Fill dropper with medication.

• Instill prescribed dosage into nostril as shown in figure 5.

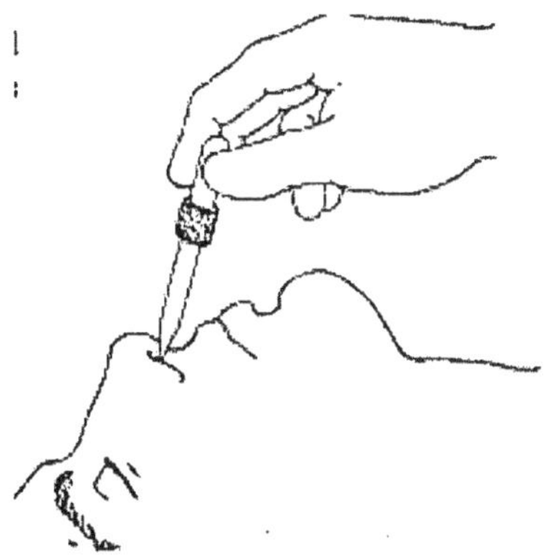

• Place tissues within easy reach.

• Keep patient in position for about 2 minutes.

SPECIAL CONSIDERATIONS

Patients should have their own properly labeled medication.

Do not permit medication to touch rubber bulb of dropper.

Avoid touching nostril with tip of dropper.

Figure 5. Instilling Nose Drops.

IV. GASTRIC TUBES

PURPOSE
To administer medications into the stomach through a tube

PROCEDURE	SPECIAL CONSIDERATIONS
• See "Guidelines for Medication Administration, General."	
• Crush all tablets and add 30 ml tap water.	
• Assemble equipment and take to bedside.	
• Elevate head of bed unless contraindicated.	Decreases risk of aspiration and regurgitation.
• Expose feeding tube.	
• Place protective pad under tubes.	

• Check stomach tube for correct placement.
   • Aspirate for gastric contents.
   • Listen with stethoscope for air entering stomach as 5 to 10 cc of air is injected into tube.
	Notify physician if tube is not placed properly.

• Attach irrigating syringe to tube with plunger removed.	
• Instill medication into irrigating syringe.	
• Follow medication with 30 ml water and allow to flow by gravity.	Ensures patient receives all medication.
• Clamp tube and cover end for 20 to 30 minutes unless contraindicated.	Allows medicine to be absorbed.
• Reattach tube to suction if indicated.	
• Rinse and clean;syringe with tap water.	
• Return syringe to bedside storage.	
• Record amount of water instilled on I&O worksheet.	
• Record medication administered on MAR.	

GASTRIC TUBES (cont)

Clamp Emesis basin Gauze sponges 4x4

SUPPLIES AND EQUIPMENT

Irrigating syringe, 60 ml Protective pad Rubber band

Sterile dressing (if ordered) Stethoscope Tap water

V. HEPARIN LOCKS

PURPOSE

To administer medications through a heparin lock

PROCEDURE	SPECIAL CONSIDERATIONS
• See "Guidelines for Medication Administration, General."	
• Assemble IV piggyback (IVPB) medication and IV administration set; attach small gauge needle to end of tubing.	
• Fill two 2 1/2 ml syringes with 2 ml normal saline.	
• Withdraw 0.9 ml normal saline and 0.1 ml heparin 1:1000 into a TB syringe.	
• Take equipment to bedside.	
• Determine patency of heparin lock. • Attach first 2 1/2 ml syringe with saline. • Aspirate and observe for blood return. • If no blood returns, check for infiltration by slowly injecting small amount of normal saline. • If infiltrated, remove heparin lock and insert new one.	
• Flush lock with 2 ml normal saline to flush out heparin.	
• Attach IVPB medication infusion set to heparin lock.	
• Administer medication.	Incompatibilities may exist resulting in a precipitate.
• Flush lock with second syringe of normal saline.	

HEPARIN LOCKS (cont)
PROCEDURE
- Flush lock with heparin solution.

- Record medication given on MAR.

SPECIAL CONSIDERATIONS

SUPPLIES AND EQUIPMENT

Alcohol sponges Heparin 1:1000

IV administration set
IVPB infusion set
Needle, 23 ga

Syringes, 2 1/2 ml (2), TB (1)

IV. INJECTIONS
A. *General*

In this section, intramuscular, intradermal, and subcutaneous injections are outlined. Many of the steps are the same for all three methods of injection. Therefore, follow the basic procedure listed below and refer to the specific procedure for special details and equipment.

PROCEDURE

- See "Guidelines for Medication Administration, General."

- Assemble equipment in preparation area.
    - Remove syringe from sterile pack.
    - Loosen the plunger by withdrawing once or twice.
- Assemble syringe and needle.

- Tighten needle.

- Score ampule with file if not prescored.

- Clean ampule or vial with antiseptic sponge and break away top of ampule.

- Discard ampule top and sponge.

- Remove needle guard and place on counter for reuse.

- Draw enough air into syringe to equal in volume the dose of medication ordered.

SPECIAL CONSIDERATIONS

See equipment list of specific procedure.

Prescored ampules are usually indicated by colored ring.

Does not apply to ampules.

INJECTIONS, GENERAL (cont)

PROCEDURE

- Insert needle into medication using aseptic technique. See figure 6.

- Withdraw slightly more medication than required dose.

- Remove needle from ampule or vial.

- Hold syringe and needle vertically.
    - Tap syringe with finger to dislodge air bubbles.
    - Aspirate to clear needle of solution.
    - Push solution up to needle hub.
    - Tip needle and syringe expelling excess solution into sink.
    - Cover and remove used needle.
    - Attach new sterile needle.
    - Read calibrations on syringe barrel at eye level to ensure correct dosage.

- Take syringe and antiseptic sponge to patient's bedside.

- Identify patient.

- Explain procedure to patient.

- Select injection site and position patient accordingly, avoiding undue exposure.

- Clean area with antiseptic sponge.

SPECIAL CONSIDERATIONS

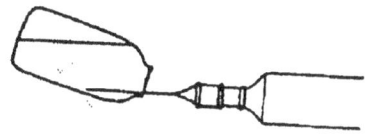

Figure 6. Withdrawing Medication from Ampule.

Do not allow solution to run down shaft of needle.

REFER TO SPECIFIC PROCEDURE: INTRAMUSCULAR, Z-TRACT, INTRADERMAL, INTRAVE-NOUS, SUBCUTANEOUS, OR INSULIN. After performing specific procedure

- Clip off needle and tip of syringe then discard.

B. *Intramuscular*
(IM)

PURPOSE
To administer <u>sterile</u> medications intramuscularly

PROCEDURE

- See "Injections, General."

- Select injection site. See figure 7.

- Position patient.
    - Place on abdomen "toeing in" for gluteal area.
    - Place on side for ventral gluteal area.

- Clean area with antiseptic sponge.

- Hold tissue taut and insert needle at 90° angle as shown in figure 8.

- Aspirate. If blood appears
    - withdraw needle
    - discard medication
    - prepare new dose
- Inject medication slowly.

- Remove needle quickly while holding skin taut.

- Place antiseptic sponge over injection site exerting slight pressure.

SPECIAL CONSIDERATIONS

Preferred site is the ventral gluteal area.

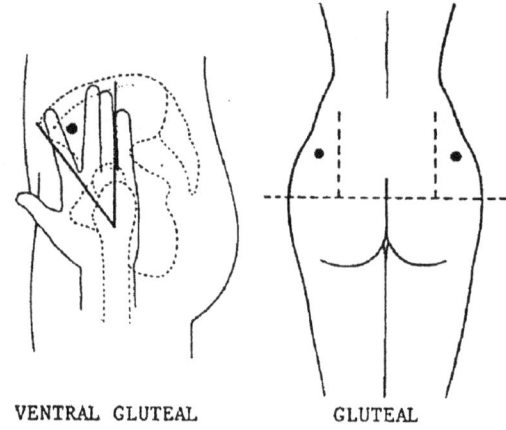

Figure 7. Intramuscular Injection Sites.

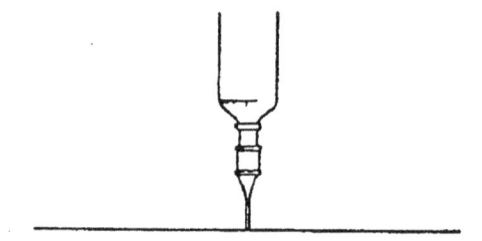

Figure 8. Intramuscular Injection Angle.

SUPPLIES AND EQUIPMENT

Antiseptic sponges (2)	Syringe, 1 to 5 ml	Needle, 21 or 22 ga, 1 1/4 ga

1. Z-Tract

PURPOSE
To prevent backflow of medication from IM injection into subcutaneous tissue

PROCEDURE	SPECIAL CONSIDERATIONS

- See "Injections, General."

- Position patient.

  - Place on abdomen "toeing in" for gluteal area.
    - Place on back for vastus lateralis area.
    - Place on side for ventral gluteal area.

- Clean area with antiseptic sponge.

- Pull skin downward or to the side and insert the needle proximal to midmuscle mass downward at an oblique angle.

- Insert needle quickly with bevel up.

- Aspirate. If blood appears
  - withdraw needle
  - discard medication
  - prepare new dose

- Inject medication slowly and empty syringe completely.

- Remove needle quickly, holding skin taut.

- Release skin and wipe area with antiseptic sponge.

C. *Intradermal*
(ID)

PURPOSE
To test for sensitivity to foreign substances

PROCEDURE	SPECIAL CONSIDERATIONS
• See "Injections, General."	Usual dose for ID testing is 0.1 ml or less.

- Select injection site.

- Clean area with antiseptic sponge.

INJECTIONS, ID (cont)

PROCEDURE	SPECIAL CONSIDERATIONS
• Grasp forearm securely on both sides of injection site. 　• Place thumb on one side and forefinger on the other. 　• Hold skin taut. • Insert needle just under skin surface at a 15° angle with bevel up. See figure 9. • Inject solution slowly to produce a bubble or wheal. • Remove needle. • Read skin test.	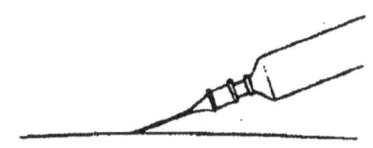 Figure 9. Intradermal Injection Angle. Do not massage. Follow local policy.

SUPPLIES AND EQUIPMENT

Antiseptic sponges (2)	Needle, 26 or 27 ga, 1 in	Syringe, TB

D. *Intravenous Piggyback*
(IVPB)

PURPOSE
　To administer medications through an IV line

PROCEDURE	SPECIAL CONSIDERATIONS
• See "Guidelines for Medication Administration, General."	
• Units with IV admixture	Pharmacy may prepare fluids with added medications.
• Check for correctness of medication as in guidelines above.	
• Units without IV admixture	
• Prepare medications and draw into syringe. 　• Obtain secondary IV solution ensuring compatibility with medication. 　• Inject medication into secondary IV solution. 　• Label solution with 　　• name of medication 　　• dosage 　　• date 　　• time 　　• your initials	Do not cover manufacturer's label.

INJECTIONS, IVPB (cont)
PROCEDURE

- Close regulator clamp on IVPB administration set.

- Insert piercing pin through stopper.

- Attach needle to tubing.

- Clear air from tubing and needle.

- Label tubing with
  - date
  - time
  - your initials

- Take equipment to bedside.

- Identify patient as in guidelines above.

- Have secondary IV on standard.
- Clean upper Y-junction on primary IV set with alcohol swab.

- Insert secondary needle into Y.

- Secure needle with tape.

- Open clamp on secondary set and adjust rate.

- Record amount of fluid infused on I&O worksheet.

- Record medication on MAR.

SPECIAL CONSIDERATIONS

Maintain aseptic technique.

Local policy dictates size of needle.

Tubing and needle must be changed every 24 hours.

Primary and secondary IVs. run simultaneously. IVPBs may not run unless primary bottle is lower. It is not necessary to adjust flow rate of primary bottle. It will begin again when IVPB is empty.

SUPPLIES AND EQUIPMENT

Adhesive tape
Alcohol swabs
IV administration set
IV solution (50 to 150 ml)
Label
Needle, 23 to 19 ga

E. *Subcutaneous* (SC)

PURPOSE
To administer medications subcutaneously

PROCEDURE
- See "Injections, General."

- Select injection site. See figure 10.

- Clean area with antiseptic sponge.

- Pinch skin between thumb and forefinger.

- Insert needle at 45° angle with bevel up as shown in figure 11.

- Aspirate. If blood appears
  - withdraw needle
  - discard medication
  - prepare new dose
- Inject medication slowly.

- Withdraw needle quickly.

- Place antiseptic sponge over site and apply gentle pressure.

SPECIAL CONSIDERATIONS

Another acceptable site is the anterior lateral aspect of the thigh.

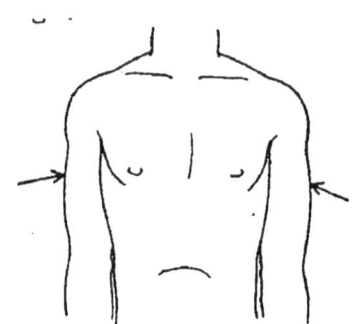

Figure 10. Subcutaneous Injection Site.

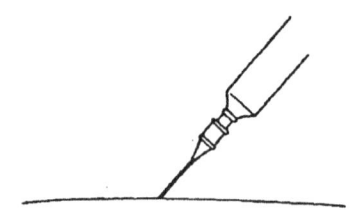

Figure 11. Subcutaneous Injection Angle.

SUPPLIES AND EQUIPMENT
Antiseptic sponges (2)   Needle, 23 ga, 3/4 in   Syringe, 2 1/2 ml

1. Insulin

PURPOSE
To lower blood sugar

PROCEDURE

- See "Injections, General."

- Roll insulin vial between palms to thoroughly mix and warm.

SPECIAL CONSIDERATIONS

INJECTIONS, SC, Insulin (cont)
PROCEDURE
• Have another person (nurse) check dose you prepare.

• Select injection site. See figure 12.
  • Rotate injection sites systematically as directed by local policy.

• Clean area with antiseptic sponge.

• Pinch skin between thumb and forefinger.

• Insert needle at 45° angle with bevel up (fig. ID.

• Aspirate. If blood appears
  • withdraw needle
  • discard medication
  • prepare new dose

• Inject medication slowly.

• Withdraw needle quickly.

• Place antiseptic sponge over site and apply gentle pressure.

Needle, 23 ga, 3/4 in

SPECIAL CONSIDERATIONS

Do not give to an NPO patient without consulting physician for specific instructions.

Absorption from the arm is more rapid than from the thigh

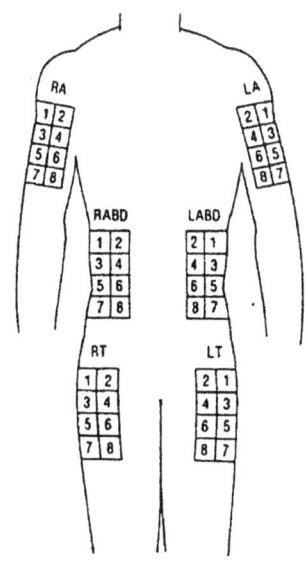

Figure 12. Insulin Injection Sites.

SUPPLIES AND EQUIPMENT
Syringe, insulin

VII. ORAL MEDICATIONS

PURPOSE
To prepare and administer medications orally

PROCEDURE

• See "Guidelines for Medication Administration, General."

SPECIAL CONSIDERATIONS

ORAL MEDICATIONS (cont)

PROCEDURE	SPECIAL CONSIDERATIONS
A. Tablets, Pills, or Capsules	
• Instruct patient how to take medication.	For example, if medication is given sublingually, let pill dissolve under toague.

• Check apical pulse rate for 1 full minute before giving cardiotonics.
  Do not give if rate is below 60 per minute.
   • Notify nurse or physician.
   • Record on MAR.	

B. Powders	
• Remove powdered medications from container with a clean, dry, tongue depressor.	
C. Liquids	
• Shake medication if it is a precipitate.	
• Remove bottle , cap and place on counter inside up.	
• Hold bottle with label covered by your palm to prevent soiling label.	
• Measure liquids at eye level using calibrated medication cup.	
• Wipe rim of bottle before recapping.	
• If medication is ordered in drops, count them aloud.	

• Dilute irons, acids, and iodides in 120 ml water and have patient drink through straw.
   • Irons and iodides stain teeth.
   •Acids and iodides can irritate mouth.	

•Give cough medications after all others are taken.	Do not dilute or give water following liquid cough medications.

VIII. SUPPOSITORIES
A. Rectal

PURPOSE
To administer medication rectally

PROCEDURE
- See "Guidelines for Medication Administration, General."

- Screen patient.

- Place patient in left Sim's position.

- Remove protective wrapper from medication.

- Don finger cot or disposable glove.

- Separate buttocks.

- Insert suppository gently through anal opening about 2 inches, using index finger.

- Have patient try to retain suppository for 20 minutes if given to cause bowel movement.

- Hold buttocks together for a minute or two to ensure absorption.

- Remove glove or finger cot and discard.

- Wash your hands.

- Assist patient to a comfortable position as needed.

SPECIAL CONSIDERATIONS

Others can be retained indefinitely.

SUPPLIES AND EQUIPMENT

Finger cot or glove

B. *Urethral*

PURPOSE
To administer medication through the urethra

PROCEDURE
- See "Guidelines for Medication Administration, General."

- Screen patient.

Females

- Place patient on back, legs drawn up and apart, with perineum exposed.

- Remove suppository from wrapper.

- Don disposable glove.

- Separate labia with thumb and forefinger and insert suppository. See figure 13.

- Remove glove and discard.

- Wash your hands.

Males

- Place patient on back with perineum exposed.

- Remove suppository from wrapper.

- Don disposable glove.

- Grasp penis with thumb and forefinger of one hand to expose meatus.

- Insert suppository.

- Remove glove and discard.

- Wash your hands.

Glove, disposable

SPECIAL CONSIDERATIONS

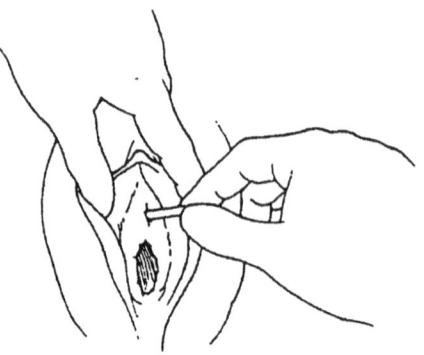

Figure 13. Inserting a Urethral Suppository.

Replace foreskin in uncircum-cised males to prevent constriction.

SUPPLIES AND EQUIPMENT

c. Vaginal

PURPOSE
To administer medication vaginally

PROCEDURE,   SPECIAL CONSIDERATIONS

- See "Guidelines for Medication Administration, General."

- Screen patient.

- Position patient in dorsal lithotomy position and expose perineum.

- Remove suppository from wrapper.

- Don disposable glove.

- Separate labia with thumb and forefinger.

- Insert suppository about 2 inches upward and backward into vagina.

- Remove glove and discard.

- Assist patient to comfortable position as needed.

- Wash your hands.

SUPPLIES AND EQUIPMENT

Finger cot or glove

www.ingramcontent.com/pod-product-compliance
Lightning Source LLC
Chambersburg PA
CBHW082042300426
44117CB00015B/2573